WOMEN'S FACTORY WORK IN WORLD WAR ONE

G.R. GRIFFITHS

The
History
Press

For Anne and Addie

Cover illustrations
Front: Women trucking steel bars. National Projectile Factory, 1918.
Back: Women painting aeroplanes using an aerograph, Austin Motor Works, 1918.
(Photographer: G.P. Lewis)

First published 2014

The History Press
The Mill, Brimscombe Port
Stroud, Gloucestershire, GL5 2QG
www.thehistorypress.co.uk

British Library Cataloguing in Publication Data.
A catalogue record for this book is available from the British Library.

ISBN 978 0 7509 5627 7

Typesetting and origination by The History Press
Printed in Great Britain

CONTENTS

ACKNOWLEDGEMENTS

This book could not have been produced without the generous help of many people and institutions. I am very grateful for the support given by the Health and Safety Executive library staff, who made available the majority of the photographs in this book.

In particular, I would like to thank Richard Lewis, Jill Gregory and Kate McNicholl for their help and interest. The staff of the Imperial War Museum were invaluable in assisting me to compare the photographs from the two archives and in tracing the background to the Women's War Work Committee. In addition, I have received help and advice from Elizabeth Roberts, Deidre Beddoe, the Southampton City Museums Oral History Project, the Manchester Studies Unit, Falkirk Museums, National Sound Archive and the Leicester Oral History Archive.

The overwhelming majority of the photographs in this book are from the archive originally held by the Home Office Industrial Museum, produced by the work of the Women's Factory Inspectorate with the Women's War Work Committee. These photographs are now in the care of the Health and Safety Inspectorate while the companion albums are held by the Imperial War Museum, although many of the photographs are not to be found in both collections.

I am most grateful for the support of The History Press in preparing this publication and especially wish to acknowledge the assistance and support of Amy Rigg.

PREFACE

The photographs presented in this book, of mainly working-class women, are drawn from a collection of many thousands of images which were commissioned in 1917 and 1918 to provide a record of the contribution to the war effort of the 6 million working women, many of whom worked in trades and professions which had been closed to them before 1914. Behind these photographs depicting the role of women supporting the war effort is the wider story of the effort to improve the working conditions of women by a small group of feminists, many of whom supported the suffrage movement before the outbreak of World War One. The research and planning undertaken in creating this record of women's work preceded later photographic documentary movements by twenty years and is linked with earlier investigations into working-class life and work such as Charles Booth's, through the membership of some of the women working in factory inspectorate.

The committee founded to oversee the creation of a record of the contribution of women to the 'home front' included two of the first senior female civil servants, Adelaide Anderson and Frances Durham, who for over a decade before the war had worked to improve the conditions and opportunities for women in society. Their membership of the Women's War Work Subcommittee enabled them to direct the photographers to produce a record of women undertaking all forms of work, some of it previously thought to be unsuitable for women, and their conditions of work.

In 1893, in the face of the unanimous opposition of the male civil servants in the Home Office Factory Inspectorate and some Trade Unions, the first female factory inspector was appointed to the Factory Inspectorate. At first only two women were appointed to inspect the entire country, which contained around 1½ million women working in industry. Adelaide Anderson saw the role of the women factory inspectors as pioneers in challenging the male-dominated civil service as well as, through their inspections, working to improve the working conditions and pay of women.

During World War One, when the occupational health of the women workers was regarded as important to war production and as a consequence to the winning of the war, the issue of health and safety in industry became a priority. The professional approach subsequently adopted by the Women's War Work Subcommittee to create a photographic archive was due to the appointment to the committee of Adelaide Anderson, Principal Lady Factory Inspector and Frances Durham, Chief Women Inspector of Employment, who recognised the opportunity of not only recording the hitherto hidden role of women in industry, but also creating a detailed record of the conditions as part of the effort to improve working conditions for women.

Thousands of photographs were eventually taken in a very short period, covering nineteen industries, based upon a statistical analysis of the production areas most affected by the substitution of men by women. The photographers were briefed by the women factory inspectors responsible for the factory, ensuring that each stage of the industrial process was recorded and that the details of working conditions were captured. In 1919, part of the archive passed to the newly founded Imperial War Museum and the remaining albums were retained by the Home Office Factory Inspectorate, who eventually used them in the Home Office Industrial Museum.

MUNITION WAGES

Earning high wages?
Yus, five quid a week.
A woman, too, mind you,
I calls it dim sweet.

Ye'are asking some questions –
But bless yer, here goes:
I spends the whole racket
On good times and clothes.

Me saving? Elijah!
Yer do think I'm mad.
I'm acting the lady,
But – I ain't living bad.

I'm having life's good times.
See 'ere, it's like this:
The 'oof come o' danger,
A touch-and-go bizz.

We're all here today, mate,
Tomorrow – perhaps dead,
If Fate tumbles on us
And blows up our shed.

Afraid! Are yer kidding?
With money to spend!
Years back I wore tatters,
Now – silk stockings, mi friend!

I've bracelets and jewellery,
Rings envied by friends;
A sergeant to swank with,
And something to lend.

I drive out in taxis,
Do theatres in style.
And this is mi verdict –
It is jolly worth while.

Worth while, for tomorrow
If I'm blown to the sky,
I'll have repaid mi wages
In death – and pass by.

Madeline Ida Bedford (1885–1956)

INTRODUCTION

The record of the impact of the 1914–18 war and the contribution of those involved in Britain and its empire is an uneven one, both between the classes and the sexes. The popular image, drawn largely from a literary record produced by the officer class, created an image that the officer class was one which suffered disproportionate losses. The detail of the statistics of losses are still disputed; however, the British Empire mobilised in the region of 9 million men, 900,000 of whom were killed and 2 million wounded, establishing a casualty rate of about 36 per cent, when the numbers of missing are included. Out of those killed, 37,000 were officers.

The table below compares the casualties suffered by the troops of the British Empire with those of some of the principal combatants.

Country	Total Mobilised Forces	Killed	Wounded	Missing	Casualties as % of forces
British Empire	9 million	0.9 million	2 million	2 million	36%
Russia	12 million	1.7 million	5 million	2.5 million	76%
France	8.4 million	1.3 million	4.2 million	5 million	73.3%
Germany	11 million	1.8 million	4.2 million	1.1 million	64.9%

At the outbreak of war, the British Army had around 710,000 men. By the time of the armistice Britain had called up 6 million men. Gradually, as the scale of casualties grew – with conscription being introduced in January 1916 for single men aged between 19 and 41 – together with the realisation of the long-term nature of the war which required the total commitment of Britain's industry to supporting the war effort, women were used to replace and work alongside men. In addition to the impact on women of working to support the war effort, the emotional impact of the losses deserves recognition; 160,000 wives lost husbands and 300,000 children lost fathers.

Packing rope in canvas for the navy, Scotland, 1918. Photographer: G.P. Lewis.

It has been estimated that at the outbreak of the war there were 3.27 million women in full-time work; working in industry, the civil service, clerical work and education. Additionally, there were 1.6 million women working in domestic service. In 1914, with the inclusion of other occupations, there were approximately 5 million women in employment, as recorded by the official statistics. This is, however, almost certainly an under estimate, as there were significant numbers of women working from home. What is evident, is that during the war, especially from early 1916, there was an increase of around 800,000 women working in industry, and an overall increase of 1 million in full-time employment. At the same time, there was a decline of 40,000 women working in domestic service as they moved to better-paid employment.

The impact of the war on women and their contribution to the war effort was unrecorded until, in 1917, a desire to create a permanent record of the military war effort led to the beginnings of the establishment of the Imperial War Museum, out of which grew a committee to record the contribution of women to the war effort. The original purpose of the movement to record the military war effort was to create a memorial in the form of a museum whose purpose was summarised as:

> to collect and preserve for public inspection objects illustrating the British share in the war. The Exhibition will comprise examples of the arms and other war materials used by the British naval and military forces, trophies captured from the enemy, souvenirs found on the battlefields, inventions connected with munition making at home, the literature and the art of the war (including regimental magazines and trench drawings), maps, the music of the war, placards issued by the Government in connexion with the recruiting, economy and war campaigns, medals and decoration, flag-day souvenirs, and autographed letters of some of those who have taken distinguished parts in the war.

In March 1917 the decision to create a National War Museum was announced and a committee was formed, headed by Sir Martin Conway, to oversee the collection of material and the acquisition of a site for the museum. Conway outlined the purpose of the museum:

> When peace returns and men are back at home, the years will pass and memory of the great days and adventures through which they lived grow dim. It's the purpose of the Museum to be a place which they can visit with their comrades, their friends, or their children, and there remember the past and behold again the great guns and other weapons with which they fought, the uniforms they wore, pictures or models of the ships and trenches and dug-outs in which weary hours were spent, or positions which they carried and ground every yard of it memorable to them.

The responsibility for the collection of material was delegated to four sub-committees, who covered the three services, and a fourth, The Women's Work Subcommittee, who covered the contribution of women to the war effort, both at home and at the front. The Women's Work Subcommittee was chaired by Lady Florence Norman, who was an active supporter of the cause for women's suffrage, through the Liberal Women's Suffrage Union. Other committee members included Lady Haig, wife of Field Marshall Douglas Haig, and Lady Margot Asquith, second wife of the former prime minister, with Sir Martin Conway's daughter, Agnes, acting as secretary.

In the first months of its work the subcommittee confined itself to the collection of material from secondary sources such as newspapers and periodicals. Contracts were agreed between the subcommittee and the leading press agencies for copies of photographs of women who had received recognition for their contribution to the war effort, usually in the areas of voluntary services and nursing. These early efforts seem to have to been limited to collecting the portraits of all the women who had either been decorated, died in the service of their country or performed outstanding deeds of valour. The majority of this material was assembled through what had been published by the newspapers.

Towards the close of 1917 a significant shift occurred in the approach and activities of the subcommittee. The appalling losses at Passchendaele (July–November 1917) forced the proposals for the museum to be reviewed by Lord Crawford, the Lord Privy Seal in Lloyd George's cabinet. Crawford, an art collector, urged that the collecting committees be far more selective in their approach. At this time the Women's Work Subcommittee was strengthened with the addition of two new members: Frances Durham (1873–1948), Chief Women Inspector of Employment at the Ministry of Labour, and Adelaide Anderson (1863–1936), Chief Lady Inspector of Factories at the Home Office. These two women, who represented the vanguard of women working in the civil service at a senior level, had the interests of women and their working conditions as their priority. Drawing upon their knowledge of women working in industry and the conditions endured, as well as the challenges of replacing the conscripted men, these two professionals immediately grasped the opportunities which the subcommittee offered them.

Working with Professor Chapman of the Board of Trade Statistical Department, Frances Durham submitted a scheme to the subcommittee for the collection of statistics for the employment of women in industry. This proposal was accepted and soon this statistical evidence was being applied by Durham and Anderson to record the levels of substitution of men by women in nineteen industries. Anderson and Durham quickly moved to persuade the subcommittee to apply this statistical evidence, as a foundation for creating a photographic record of the 'significant' areas of industry where the substitution of women for men had taken place. Early in 1918 the subcommittee reported that:

In co-operation with the Chief Lady Inspector of Factories the Women's War Work Sub-Committee is at work on the formation of a series of photographs for record purposes which shall show the most important processes in which women have acted as a substitute for men in the factories since the war.

Anderson and Durham understood that they had an opportunity to not only record the contribution of women to the war effort through their work in industry, but also to further their broader concerns in recording and improving the conditions for women who were frequently working in hazardous conditions. They moved quickly and on 20 August 1918 two photographers from the Department of Information were seconded to the Women's Work Subcommittee: Horace Nicholls and G.P. Lewis.

Horace Nicholls had been employed from 1917 by the Department of Information as the official 'home front' photographer. His photographs were mainly used for the propaganda campaign overseas, which was largely directed towards the United States. Nicholls was a very fine photographer who had made his name as a photojournalist during the Boer War and, on his return, had specialised in photographing Edwardian life. Very little is known of Nicholls's colleague, George Parnham Lewis, who was also a fine photographer; he worked on the project to record women's work in industry in 1918, travelling throughout Britain, and then disappears almost without trace.

As soon as the two photographers were seconded to them in August 1918, Durham and Anderson drew upon their statistical evidence to quickly organise the recording of the industries in which women played a significant role. Horace Nicholls worked mainly around London while G.P. Lewis covered the industries outside the capital. Lewis's visits to the factories were organised through the Women's Factory Inspectorate, a woman factory inspector briefing him on the stages of the industrial production and working conditions to be photographed and recorded. Particular attention was paid to producing a record of all aspects of working in a factory, with many of the photographs taken to illustrate points of health and safety.

Lewis, in particular, produced some strikingly 'natural' photographs that very effectively recorded the dirty and heavy work undertaken by women. The range of industries covered by this ambitious documentary project in a short time was remarkable. In one trip lasting a fortnight, Lewis recorded the work of women in the chemical, flour, rubber, asbestos, glucose, India rubber, aluminium, paint, dye and munition industries. In less than four months Lewis took over 1,300 photographs and Nicholls nearly 2,000. Within two months the volume of photographs taken was such as to enable the Women's War Work Subcommittee to hold an exhibition on women's war work, held at the Whitechapel Art Gallery in London. The success of the exhibition, which attracted 82,000 visitors, indicated the degree to which the general public were ignorant of the industrial work being performed by women, due to the domestic press censorship.

Towards the end of 1918 Lewis left the project and the committee reviewed the progress made in producing a record of the contribution of women to the war effort. An obvious gap was the work of women in France which, with the cessation of hostilities, the committee was eager to record. Although Horace Nicholls was still working for them, it is interesting that the subcommittee chose to appoint a woman, the photographer Olive Edis (1876–1955), to carry out the commission. Edis, a recognised studio portraitist before the war, began work in March 1919, photographing the work of women who were in France working for the Red Cross, the YWCA and the Voluntary Aid Detachment, as demobilisation continued throughout 1919. Edis brought a new depth to the project record:

Edis was photographing something new, not only to her in terms of photographic practice, but also to the women who were her subjects. Their excitement and energy emerges clearly in the many portraits which Edis produced ... her war workers have a grace and presence which speaks of their confidence as skilled and informed women ... the central theme of her work is a documentary of busy accomplished women. (*Dictionary of National Biography*)

On the completion of Olive Edis's work in France in 1919, the Women's War Work Subcommittee was disbanded. The photographic archive, containing thousands of images, was divided between the new photographic archive of the Imperial War Museum and the Home Office's Factory Department, where Adelaide Anderson headed the Women's Factory Inspectorate. The Home Office's collection was subsequently passed, in 1927, to the new Home Office Industrial Museum. This museum was established to 'promote the safety, health and welfare of industrial workers'. Opening on 3 December 1927 in Horseferry Road, Westminster, the museum became the Safety, Health and Welfare Museum in 1947, closing in 1978. Its archive passed to the Health and Safety Executive.

Women trolleying crushed silica stone, South Wales, 1918.

As early as 1910 the concept of a museum which would demonstrate the latest techniques of safety and welfare was approved by the Treasury, based upon similar museums in Milan, Berlin, Munich, Amsterdam, Paris and Lausanne which had been in existence since the beginning of the century under the name of ' Workmen's Welfare Museums'. When war broke out in 1914, the museum building was already completed, incorporating the latest safety features in its design, but its opening was postponed until 1927. Influential in creating a movement for the foundation of the museum was the *Daily News'* 'Sweated Industries Exhibition', held in the Queen's Hall, London in 1906. Among the key organisers of the exhibition were Mary MacArthur of the Women's Trade Union League and Margaret Macdonald of the Women's Industrial Council, both of whom were closely involved with the Women's Factory Inspectorate before World War One.

When the museum opened it had a floor space of around 10,000 square feet, in which the approved techniques for protecting the industrial worker against accidents were demonstrated, together with examples of the necessary conditions for promotion of the health and welfare of the workforce. The museum was run by an inspector from the engineering section of the factory inspectorate, with an emphasis upon the use of working exhibits. The safety features included within the building's design were the latest examples of modern lighting, heating and ventilation, as well as new features such as non-slip treads and a vacuum cleaning plant. The intention was that the museum would be used by trade unions, manufacturing associations, medical schools and technical colleges, as well as the designers of factories, machinery and power plants and manufacturers of machinery guards and other protective appliances. The factory inspectorate also used the museum as a training centre where the principals of industrial safety were taught; within the museum there was a lecture theatre and cinema.

The task of the museum was to impress upon the visitor, whatever their connection with industry or the workplace, the terrible level of industrial injuries. To do this the museum displayed a comparison of World War One casualties in its gallery:

World War I 1914–1918	British Industry 1919–1924
British wounded 1,693,262	Industrial injuries 2,385,766 (killed 20,263)

An important part of the museum was its photographic and film archive, which contained many photographs taken by the factory inspectors as they recorded the wide range of working conditions they encountered. At the heart of the archive was the founding collection of photographs taken during World War One.

THE WOMEN'S FACTORY INSPECTORATE

From 1833 male factory inspectors, based in the Home Office, had enforced the Factory Acts. In 1842 a law forbidding the employment of women underground in the mining industries was passed, followed by the 1847 Ten Hours Act which limited the workday of women and children in the textile industry. In 1867 the reach of the Ten Hours Act was extended to cover all factories employing more than fifty. Many organisations concerned with women's welfare and rights feared that the protective legislation would result in unemployment for women, which it initially did in many industries. The Women's Provident and Protective League (later to become the Women's Trade Union League) opposed the protective legislation, arguing that it would severely restrict job opportunities for women. However, following the 1847 Act, the League decided that if the protective legislation was to be effective, women had to be involved in the inspection of factories.

From the beginning, there was a debate about not only the principle of women inspectors, but also from which class the women should be drawn. There was initially opposition from some trade unions to the appointment of working-class women to positions of authority in factories where men were employed. However, these objections were defeated through a number of resolutions carried in 1878 by the Trade Union Congress (TUC). The need for women inspectors was pressed because it was felt that 'men inspectors could not enter into or understand the women's feelings, necessities, and sympathies'. The TUC argued for the appointment of women as factory inspectors, 'who should be women – not ladies, but practical working women'.

Gradually, the demands for a separate women's inspectorate grew; in 1881 Lord Shaftesbury chaired a conference on the subject and in 1890 the London Women's Trade Council made representations to the Home Office insisting that only women inspectors could effectively inspect working conditions where the majority of the workforce were women. Again, the point was made that the inspector had to be a woman with the practical experience of workroom life. In 1892, the demand for women inspectors was again pressed by the Women's Trade Union Association letter to the Home Office, arguing that 'women are better able to judge than men of the conditions under which women can work safely among machinery'.

Finally, in 1892 the Royal Commission on Labour recommended that more factory inspectors needed to be appointed to enforce the legislation on the conditions of employment in factories and that women should be appointed amongst the new inspectors. In January 1893, Herbert Asquith announced that two women inspectors would be appointed. (Asquith's wife, a member of the Women's War Work Subcommittee, would later work with Adelaide Anderson, the

Women washing the insides of the steel-ingot moulds before use, National Projectile Factory, Hackney Marshes, London, 1918.

Chief Lady Inspector of Factories, on the recording of women's factory war work.) The women appointed were not drawn from the working class and were called lady inspectors. The first 'Lady Factory Inspector', May Abraham, was appointed in 1893, together with Mary Muirhead Paterson. May Abraham had been secretary to Emilia Dilke, the leader of the Women's Trade Union League, and worked in the inspectorate until the birth of her son in 1897. The success of the first two appointments led to two further appointments a year later of Lucy Deane and Adelaide Anderson. The four women were responsible for 144,000 factories and workshops employing 1,403,568 women and girls.

Adelaide Anderson, who had worked for the Royal Commission on Labour, became Chief Lady Inspector in 1897. Anderson was born in Australia to a Scottish shipbroker who returned to Britain for her education, where she went to Girton College, Cambridge. Before working for the Royal Commission, she worked for the Women's Co-operative Guild, lecturing on economics and philosophy. She joined the staff of the Royal Commission in 1892 and the factory inspectorate in 1894.

The initial work of the factory inspectorate was by no means limited to the inspection and correction of conditions in the industrial workplace. Adelaide Anderson placed equal importance on the collection of data to support the amendment of existing rules and to assist with the passage of new legislation. It is clear that the women inspectors viewed the collection of statistics as an essential part of the approach to understanding and improving the conditions of working women through supplying evidence for future legislation. This approach was echoed in the founding resolution of the Women's Industrial Council (established 1894), which had close links with founding members of the Women's Factory Inspectorate:

> In the opinion of this conference it is desirable that a central council shall be established to organize special and systematic inquiry in to the conditions of working women, to provide accurate information concerning those interests, and promote such action as may seem conducive to their improvement.

To achieve this the council would 'investigate the actual facts of women's work, and collect and publish trustworthy information about the conditions of their employment'.

This interest in social issues and the recording of social conditions dated back to the 1840s. A passion for the quantification of the living and working conditions of the working class accompanied the interest in social investigation. During the same period, statistics as a science grew. The Board of Trade set up a statistical office in 1832, the British Association founded a statistical section in 1833 and, in the same year, statistical societies were founded in Manchester and London.

Charles Booth's *Life and Labour of the People in London*, the first volume of which was published in 1889, opened an era of statistical social research which grew out of Booth's desire to create 'a large statistical framework which is built to receive accumulations of facts out of which is at last evolved the theory and the law and the basis for more intelligent action'.

The Women's Factory Inspectorate had close links with this movement for social investigation. May Abraham and Adelaide Anderson worked for the Royal Commission of Labour with Clara Collet, who had previously worked with Charles Booth as an investigator into the conditions of women's work in the East End of London. Seebohm Rowntree, who carried out his own survey of poverty in York (1899) inspired by Booth's work in London, worked closely with the Women's Factory Inspectorate throughout World War One on women's welfare in industry. A further link between the late nineteenth-century social survey movement and the Women's Factory Inspectorate was provided by Sir Hubert Llewellyn Smith, who was a contemporary of Seebohm Rowntree and in 1928 was director of the committee that undertook the 'New Survey of London Life

Building rubber treads for tyres, Charles Makintosh and Sons Ltd, Manchester, September 1918. Photographer: G.P. Lewis.

and Labour', updating Booth's work. Llewellyn Smith had been a member of Booth's original team of investigators and later joined the Board of Trade and the Ministry of Labour, where during World War One he worked closely with the Women's Factory Inspectorate, analysing the extent to which women were replacing men in industry.

Although severely understaffed, the annual reports for the first years of the Women's Factory Inspectorate show the women inspectors enforcing protective legislation, paying particular attention to excessive hours, poor sanitation, dangerous practices, illegal stoppages of wages, payment in kind and the exploitation of child labour. The female inspectors worked separately from their male counterparts, although gradually the organisation of the Women's Inspectorate came to mirror the male inspectorate. In the early years the women inspectors worked from London, and were not assigned to regions. Within ten years, the women inspectors were assigned to a particular region, like their male colleagues – greatly improving their knowledge of an area and its industries, which was subsequently drawn upon by the visiting photographers of the Women's War Subcommittee.

Up to World War One, the Women and Men's Inspectorates remained separate. During the war, as in the factories, women gradually replaced men as factory inspectors and inspected workplaces irrespective of the numbers of men or women employed. In 1897 there were five women inspectors; by the outbreak of the war there were twenty-one, and by 1921 there were forty-two women inspectors and 195 men inspectors. The success of women inspectors' substitution for men inspectors during the war led to the demise in 1921 of the women's branch, when an integrated factory inspectorate was created.

WORLD WAR ONE

World War One transformed the British economy; in August 1914 no one anticipated the scale and length of the war and its consequent impact upon the British economy and society. In 1924 the growing tensions in the war economy were summarised:

> Throughout the war there were two phrases which must have been repeated hundreds of times … 'Every private interest must be subordinated to the successful prosecution of the war' and 'There must be as little interference as possible with the normal channels of trade' … The real problem was to determine the exact degree of interference with normal trade channels that was necessary for the successful prosecution of the war. (E.M.H. Lloyd, Experiments in State Control)

Year by year, as the war continued and the war effort expanded to embrace all parts of the economy, the tension between the desire to continue with 'business as usual' and the requirement for co-ordinated state intervention grew.

The immediate effect of the outbreak of war was an increase in unemployment. Many of the industries worst hit were those which in peacetime employed large numbers of women. In dressmaking only 34 per cent of women were in full-time employment; in boots and shoes a mere 13 per cent of women workers were full-time. To mitigate this position a Central Committee on Women's Employment under Mary MacArthur, who in 1905 had been involved the organisation of the Sweated Industries Exhibition, was established to organise relief work for women. The Central Committee was advised by the Chief Lady Inspector of Factories, Adelaide Anderson, while local committees were supported by the local women's factory inspectorate.

Within twelve months the pendulum swung the other way; there was a shortage of skilled labour as the war created a demand in the industries which traditionally employed women. 'Substitution', the extensive use of women in the place of men in industry, began on a limited scale in the summer of 1915. It quickly accelerated the following year with the introduction of conscription for men in January 1916, and women increasingly replaced men throughout the economy. During the war the number of women employed in industry increased by over 1½ million, with approximately 700,000 replacing men. The rise in the female share of industrial employment increased from 26 per cent to 36 per cent. In some industries the replacement of men was remarkable. In the metal and engineering industries the female share of the labour force rose from 9.4 per cent to 24.6 per cent, while in the chemical industry it rose from 20.1 per cent to 39.0 per cent and in what was defined as the government establishments (munitions factories) it rose from 2.6 per cent to 46.7 per cent.

As the demand to meet production quotas grew it became unpatriotic to talk about limiting hours of work or be too demanding about safety. The Home Office permitted the relaxation of the Factory Acts and shift work, long hours, Sunday work and shorter mealtimes all became the norm. Sylvia Pankhurst took up the matter of the long hours and poor conditions that women worked under:

> Sometimes a woman wrote to me, broken down in health by overwork, complaining of long walks over sodden, impromptu tracks, ankle deep in mud to newly-erected factories; of night shifts spent without even the possibility of getting a drink of water; of workers obliged to take their meals amidst the dust and fumes of the workshop. (*The Home Front*, 1932)

Concern about the conditions of work for women led the Ministry of Munitions to establish a commission to 'consider and advise on the questions of industrial fatigue, hours of labour, and other matters affecting the personal health and physical efficiency of workers in munition factories and workshops'. Working with Seebohm Rowntree who was a member of the commission, the women inspectors supplied Rowntree with 1,396 surveys of the conditions in factories which employed nearly 200,000 women. The results were classified by the women factory inspectors 'according to the degree of urgency' for his attention: 31 per cent of the factories were regarded as acceptable; 49 per cent of the factories were rated as second class, and 20 per cent were rated as third class as they lacked adequate meal rooms, washing and first-aid facilities, rest rooms and 'suitable supervision'.

During the period, as the numbers of women employed in industry rose the numbers employed in domestic service declined, over 400,000 leaving the industry. Surprisingly, despite the increased employment of women in many industries during the war, there appears to have been no long-term effect on the overall level of female participation in the workforce. The 1921 Census records 25.4 per cent of women as employed, the same proportion as in 1911. The increased employment of women in the clerical trades, engineering and the civil service were more than offset by falling levels of employment in the traditionally

Steel shell bars being cut by circular saws. Note the absence of protection for the hands or face.

A basic mess room in a munitions factory, 1918.

female industries such as textiles and clothing. After 1918, there was pressure for the women to leave the industries in which they had replaced conscripted men.

The growth of women's employment in industry during the war is shown by the table below:

Employment of Women in Industry 1914–18

Trade	Estimated number of women employed			% of females in the workforce	
	July 1914	*July 1918*	*Difference*	*1914*	*1918*
Metals	170,000	594,000	+424,000	9	25
Chemical	40,000	104,000	+64,000	20	39
Textile	863,000	827,000	−36,000	58	67
Clothing	612,000	563,000	−44,000	68	76
Food/Drink	196,000	235,000	+39,000	35	49
Paper/Printing	147,000	141,000	6,000	36	48
Wood	44,000	79,000	+35,000	15	32
China/Earthenware	32,000	197,000	+93,000	4	10
Leather	23,000				
Other	49,000				
Govt Establishments	2,000	225,000	+223,000	3	47
TOTAL	2,178,600	2,970,000	+ 792,000	36	37

(Taken from the Report of the War Cabinet Committee on Women in Industry, 1919)

At the time of the outbreak of World War One the nature of women's employment was already changing. New opportunities for women in the fields of clerical, shop and factory work offered higher wages and shorter and more regular hours than those enjoyed by women employed as domestic servants, which was by far the largest occupation for women until the war. Until 1914 the number of domestic servants was still growing, although at a slackening rate compared with the closing decades of the nineteenth century. During World War One the proportion of women in factory work rose rapidly with the introduction of conscription for men in 1916. By the end of the war the number of women munitions workers had risen from 2,000 to 225,000, while the number of female domestic servants had fallen from 1,658,000 to 1,250,000. After the war there was, according to government reports, a growing distaste amongst girls regarding entering domestic service under its present conditions, and a reluctance on the part of parents to allow their daughters to enter service. As domestic service declined in popularity among younger women, the average age of those employed in service rose. In 1891, 40 per cent of those employed in service were below 20; by the outbreak of World War Two over 50 per cent were aged between 35 and 55.

Percentage of working women employed as domestic servants, 1881–1931

Year	Percentage in domestic service
1881	44
1901	40
1911	34.5
1931	24

During the period 1914–18 there were broadly three stages in the development of women's employment in industry:

i) The expansion of women's work within trades which were traditionally major employers of women: textiles and clothing.

ii) The substitution of women in many male occupations to release men for the forces.

iii) The concentration of women in government munitions factories, frequently newly built.

With the outbreak of war, the immediate effect upon women's employment was to create unemployment on a widespread scale, particularly in industries associated with women:

At the beginning of the war a London firm of theatrical costumiers in a large way of business wrote to ask if I could help them to find some work which would enable them to keep their staff of nearly 200 women employed. Orders in their own trade had entirely failed owing to there being no new productions at the theatres, and pantomime orders being cancelled. I advised them where to apply, and eventually they secured a War Office contract for khaki uniforms and a sub-contract for shirts, and the empty workrooms were once more in full work.

The same weekly wages were paid as when the workers were on theatrical costumes, but the firm were content for the time being to make no profit rather than that their staff should be disbanded and the factory closed down.

The furriers were found to be suffering severely at the outbreak of the war; the early autumn would, normally, find all this industry busy preparing the winter goods: ladies' muffs and neckwear, fur coats and linings for men and ladies' wear. But on the day after the declaration of war orders from wholesale houses were cancelled and the retailers' demand ceased. Relief came to this trade early in October with the placing of orders from the War Office for fur and skin coats for the troops. Immediately all furriers were fully occupied, and a shortage of fur sewers and machinists became a serious difficulty in the execution of the contract. (Women's Factory Inspector Report, 1915)

The Women's Factory Inspectorate noted that 'the phase of unemployment and short time, following immediately on the sudden alarm and shock of war, was felt throughout our industries and by almost all workers to some degree, but most intensely of all and for the longest time by women.'

Towards the end of 1914 some industries expanded rapidly as they received orders to supply the forces:

the large trades involving women, in which there was an incessant, increasing demand for their labour, are woollen and worsted textiles (khaki, flannel,

Grinding bases of grenades, Castlelaurie Foundry, Falkirk Iron Company, 1917.

blankets); hosiery clothing (military tailoring and fur coat making cap making shirt making); boots and shoes and other leather articles ... surgical dressing and bandages, tin canister and box making. (Annual Report, 1914)

The annual report for 1915 noted that Miss Taylor, a factory inspector whose district included the important clothing trade area of Leeds, reported:

that the pressure of work consequent on the demand for uniforms has precipitated a change which has slowly been taking place throughout the year, that is the gradual conversion of workshops into factories.

During the last three months of the year the demand for soldiers' and sailors' clothing has exceeded the amount the combined forces of the trade can supply. At the same time the demand for civilians' clothing was very small. The nature of the khaki work makes it impossible for places equipped only with treadle machines to turn it out at remunerative prices. Therefore, unless they are to be continually out of work it becomes necessary to fit power to their machines. April and May have hitherto been the months when the notification of new factories was heaviest. The notifications for the last six weeks have been exactly double what they were in April and May. Since the beginning of the war 45 new clothing factories have been added to the registers on a total of 420. Whether this increase is likely to be permanent it is impossible to say. One of the most important industries in which occupiers in Glasgow and other districts have adapted themselves to new conditions is that of carpet making, some of the looms in several carpet factories having been successfully adapted to the weaving of Army blankets.

Another instance of industrial development was in a canvas bag factory where a number of women, girls and men have, since the outbreak of war, been employed in the making of nosebags for horses, engaged in sewing the bottoms to the bags. In two factories, in one of which hosiery is manufactured and in the other Army uniforms, additional British labour being unavailable, the management have taken on a few Belgian women and girls. (Factory Inspector's Report, 1915)

The demands of the war economy did not necessarily bring improvements in conditions of employment or wages for women. *The Women's Dreadnought* in 1914 published allegations that women working for government contractors were working at sweated rates of pay:

Jameson's of Poplar, Government contractors, pay women 2s. 1d. a dozen for making soldiers' shirts. One woman who has been making boys' shirts for 2s. 6d. a dozen, to be sold to private firms, tells us that she refused Government work until there was no more private work to do. She tells us that the soldiers' shirts, besides being paid at lower rates, are larger and more complicated than others, and are of harsh stuff that makes the women's fingers sore. The shirts are dark and the cotton black, and the work therefore tries the eyes a good deal. The women can only manage to do a dozen shirts a day, by working very hard and out of the 2s. 1d. they earn by this, they have to pay 2d 1/2d. a reel for cotton – a reel does not do quite a dozen shirts …

… strange patriotism this, that allows the Government contractors who are making money out of this war to sweat the women workers in this disgraceful fashion.

In March 1915 the government took steps to create a register of women who were willing to undertake war work. The response was immediate and within six months over 110,000 women had registered. However, prejudice against the employment of women restricted the numbers of women who were found employment through the register to 5,000. This deeply ingrained prejudice against the employment of women outside their traditional areas of work was only broken in late 1915 when the shortage of munitions forced the government to establish a Ministry of Munitions, which encouraged the employment of women in the munitions factories; these were declared 'controlled establishments' and so fell outside trade union restrictive practices. Employment in the munitions factories was generally better paid than in most industries, and as women moved away from their traditional areas of employment into the better paid munitions work, a shortage of labour was created in the clothing and textile industries towards the end of 1915. The shortage of women in textiles became so acute that some Lancashire textile manufactures asked for the school leaving age be reduced to 12.

The reorganisation of munition production by the Ministry of Munitions, which could legally enforce the suspension of trade union practices, paved the way for the large-scale mobilisation of women in other industries. 'Dilution officers' were appointed to increase and encourage the dilution of male labour into factories. The dilution officer visited factories in order to assess the amount of labour required and how production could be met by using female labour wherever possible. A further impetus to the use of women was given in January 1916 when conscription for single men was introduced, followed by the introduction of universal conscription. The rapid introduction of women into the labour force is indicated by the employment of over half a million new women in munitions work between July 1915 and July 1916. Munitions work became far more popular among women than the traditional women's trades; the Women's Factory Inspectorate reported in 1915: 'The difficulty at present is in the replacement of women who have left the so called women's and lower-

Women trimming stockings and gloves. Following the recession which succeeded the declaration of war, there was a huge rise in the demand for woollen goods as the trench warfare moved into stalemate.

paid industry to take a hand in work formerly done by men'. Large numbers of domestic servants grasped the opportunity to escape 'service', as was reported by *Domestic News*:

> With the coming of the war domestic workers in large numbers gave up their work for other occupations and it was not all patriotism that prompted them, rather a desire to escape a condition of employment that was distasteful to them on account … of what may be termed the bondage of domestic service.

The overwhelming majority of the women working in industry were working class. Monica Cosens, a middle-class volunteer for munitions work, estimated that only 9 per cent of munitions workers were middle class. Her memories of work in a munitions factory convey a sense of isolation: 'Frankly I did not like the look of my companions. They were rough, loud voiced and gave me the impression of being ill-natured and having sharp tongues.'

Forming the patterns on jacquard cards for lace production, Nottingham, 1918.
Photographer: G.P. Lewis.

The growth in munitions employment during 1916 and 1917 was paralleled by the substitution of men by women in other industries during the same period. Increasingly women replaced men in industries such as chemicals, building, metalworking, food and the ship and aircraft industries. By 1917 the *Labour Gazette* was estimating that a third of working women were replacing male workers. The trade unions saw women as a threat to their wage rates and pre-war conditions of employment. Initially, the unions attempted to restrict the areas of employment for women.

However, when the process of substitution could no longer be resisted, the trade unions argued that women should be paid the same rates as men in order to prevent women undercutting the men's rates. This gave rise to the Treasury Agreement, which was a contract between the government and the unions whereby the unions were promised that skilled men's rates would be maintained and that women replacing them would receive the full rate. In addition, agreement was reached that after the war the industries should return to pre-war conditions and the agreements would not lead to any permanent substitution of men by women, and the semi-skilled or female labour would be the first to be discharged when hostilities ceased.

Although a range of agreements were made on the use of women throughout the war, opposition to women being employed in industries previously dominated by men continued and took many forms. A woman tool fitter reported several instances of harassment by her fellow male workers: 'My drawer was nailed up by the men, and oil was poured over everything through a crack another night.' Another woman, employed in an engineering works, recalled: 'I was sacked. There was a man who chewed tobacco and kept spitting in my pocket and I hit him.'

There is little doubt that the women had to contend with the strong feeling, largely shared by the employer and the male workers, that they had no business to be in the factories at all. Throughout the war there was concern over what the effects of industrial employment upon the women would be. Reports ranged from the transformation of once strong and healthy women into 'pale and anaemic creatures with no vitality and no joy in living' to patriotic descriptions of

Women painting
aeroplanes using an
aerograph (a mechanical
paint-spraying
machine), Austin Motor
Works, Northfield,
near Birmingham,
1918. Photographer:
G.P. Lewis.

women whose hard work 'does not seem to be doing much harm to their health for their eyes are bright, their cheeks are fresh and there is hardly any evidence of fatigue among them'.

Reviewing the effect of wartime employment upon women, the War Cabinet Committee's Report on Women in Industry reported that they considered women's health had improved during the war due to improved health care, nutrition and physical work. In her evidence to the War Cabinet Committee Dr Janet Campbell submitted that an improvement in the standards of women's health had occurred during the war years. Prior to the war, malnutrition had been one of the main causes of ill-health, anaemia and stunted physique among women. Campbell's observations were supported by Mary MacArthur, who maintained before the war:

> Women are more liable to incapacity by sickness than men and it is my contention that (apart from normal physical reasons) this extra sickness in women is due to their greater poverty and to the character of their employment.
>
> Long hours, long standing, lack of fresh air, long intervals without food, are undeniably, especially in the case of young anaemic girls, detrimental to health and the low wages which attach to most women's employment involve insufficient and often improper food.

Before the War Cabinet Committee in 1919, Dr Mary Deacon of the National Amatol Factory in Liverpool reported that in her experience of looking at over 7,000 women and 1,000 men, she found that 'men could not work longer, though they could do heavier work … women had a higher standard of factory hygiene than men.' She found 'no grounds that women grew more fatigued than men and so had more accidents. Women who worked at night could not get proper sleep at daytime and this contributed to minor ailments. No gynaecological trouble was caused by women working in factories.'

Working in munitions factories and other industries did involve risks to the health of the workers who handled chemicals such as TNT. Women working with explosives developed such symptoms as coughing, swellings, burns and eruptions on the skin. During the first two years of the war, inexperience of the dangers of working with TNT led to over 100 fatalities from TNT poisoning, as well as many serious illnesses. An investigation by the Home Office led to a new set of regulations on the safety and health of munitions workers which included clauses about cleanliness, ventilation, washing facilities, the provision of free milk, special uniforms and the appointment of full-time medical officers. Industrial processes other than munitions also involved hazards to health; for example, women working in foundries suffered from the fumes. According to a female foundary worker active in 1916–17: 'We had to see a doctor once a month … because there were fumes and we had to wear masks. We were allowed a pint of milk a day … we used to have two hours up (in a crane) and two hours down, we had to rest, you see.'

Alongside the concern for the health of women working in industry was official alarm at the falling birth-rate creating a sense of urgency to establish an infant and child welfare system. The increased concern for infant welfare was expressed in a number of campaigns throughout the war, one of which was 'National Baby Week', held in July 1917. The week was opened by Queen Mary, who was received by a guard of honour made up of 120 mothers and babies. Certainly the war did stimulate an interest in how child welfare services could be improved: in 1914 local authorities employed 600 health visitors; this soared to 2,577 by 1918. Similarly, the number of child welfare centres rose from 350 in 1914 to 578 by 1918. Reviewing the creation of the School Medical Service the Chief Medical Officer to the Board of Education wryly noted:

The School Medical Service has emerged from the War … bearing not only evidences of the struggle, but also the complete vindication for its existence and of its recognition as the educational portion of a national system of Preventive Medicine. The returns of the medical examinations of recruits to HM Forces, and their import in connection with recruitment and the national physique,

Pottery kiln being loaded prior to firing, Stoke-on-Trent, 1918.

directed public attention to the findings and results of the School Medical Service, and drove home the lesson that the nation was suffering from its neglect to detect their development into physical disability. As a result of the war there has arisen a new conception of the value of the child to the nation.

Women at Munition Making

Their hands should minister unto the flame of life,
Their fingers guide
The rosy teat, swelling with milk,
To the eager mouth of the suckling babe
Or smooth with tenderness,
Softly and soothingly,
The heated brow of the ailing child.
Or stray among the curls
Of the boy or girl, thrilling to mother love.
But now,
Their hands, their fingers
Are coarsened in munition factories.
Their thoughts, which should fly
Like bees among the sweetest mind flowers
Gaining nourishment for the thoughts to be,
Are bruised against the law,
'Kill, kill'.
They must take part in defacing and destroying the natural body
Which, certainly during this dispensation
Is the shrine of the spirit.
O God!
Throughout the ages we have seen,
Again and again
Men by Thee created
Cancelling each other.
And we have marvelled at the seeming annihilation
Of Thy work.
But this goes further,
Taints the fountain head,
Mounts like a poison to the Creator's very heart.
O God!
Must It anew be sacrificed on earth?

Mary Gabrielle Collins (1874–1945)

WOMEN v. MEN

The wartime conditions provided an unexpected opportunity to test assumptions about women's employment, by placing women in jobs previously held by men. Prior to the war it had been assumed that women could only perform certain kinds of work: light, sedentary, indoor work, especially labour which did not require a high degree of strength or skill, intellectual or physical.

There was consensus before 1914 that only the relative cheapness of women's labour offered any inducement to an employer to employ women in preference to men. The demands of industry during the war put these assumptions to the test. Following the war there were attempts to review the performance of women by various employer federations who found that overall their fears about the unsuitability of women for industrial employment were unfounded. In many areas women performed better than men, taking on jobs or occupations which normally required a term of apprenticeship which would exceed the period of the war. The ability of women to acquire skills considerably faster than the normal apprenticeship period had the effect of undermining the apprenticeship system, as Walter Greenwood noted in *Love on the Dole* (1933):

> 'You're part of a graft, Harry;' he said: 'All Marlowe's want is cheap labour; the apprentice racket is one of their ways of getting it. Nobody teach you anything simply because there's so little to be learnt. You'll pick up all you require by asking questions and watching others work … Your apprenticeship's a swindle, Harry. The men they turn out think they're engineers same as they do at all the other places, but they're only machine minders. Don't you remember the women in the war?'
>
> 'What women?' Harry asked, troubled by what Larry had said.
>
> 'The women who took the places of the engineers who'd all served their time. The women picked up straight away what Marlowe's and others say it takes seven years' apprenticeship to learn.

In addition to having to learn their skills quickly, outside the normal apprenticeship scheme, women had to combat reluctance on the part of skilled men to teach women:

> In every industrial district without exception, there was continuous opposition to the introduction of women. In some cases this opposition was overt to the point of striking; in other instances … it took the insidious form of refusal to instruct women, or attempt to restrict the scope of their work or to discredit their efforts. (Home Office Report, 1919)

Female construction workers on the site of a new aircraft factory for Jolly's, Birmingham.

These and other disadvantages were to some degree counterbalanced by the introduction of new labour-saving devices and machines during the war.

The substitution of men by women led to a series of agreements between the government and the trade unions defining under what conditions substituted labour could be taken on. These agreements formed the basis of the Treasury Agreement of March 1915 and were incorporated into the Munitions of War Act 1915. This agreement between the government, employers' associations and trade unions included the following provisions:

i)   The rate customarily paid for a job should not be lowered on the importation of a different type of labour (whether that of women, unskilled men or juveniles).

ii) That the suspension of restrictions on such other types of labour hold good only for the duration of the war, or till such time as sufficient male labour should be again available.

The trade unions' attitude towards the employment of women, in part dictated by men's ideas as to what work it was 'proper and decent' for women to perform, had also been influenced by fear of the effects of women competing with men in occupations traditionally undertaken by men.

The quality and value of the contribution of women to the 'Home Front' was summarised by the Home Office after the war:

> The opinion of the Factory Department is recorded that the substitution (of women for men in industry during the war) has proved successful in a great majority of cases; that women have shown capacity to take up many of the more skilled processes hitherto reserved for men and to carry them out completely and well, and have displayed unexpected readiness for work which at first sight seemed wholly unsuitable for them.

Commenting upon the division of duties and work which had occurred before the war, the report further noted:

> Occupations with demarcation between men's and women's work or duties … cover the bulk of the occupations in industry proper. Though often the lines of demarcation are artificial, it is rarely that they do not exist … There are many cases where women's work in one district or factory, is men's in another district or factory. (War Cabinet Committee, 1919)

Collecting evidence on the quality of the work performed by women, the Home Office received submissions from most industries, including the Federation of Master Printers who, in a number of cases, paid women less than men, although their output was higher. The employers' reasoning for this inequality was that the women's output might fall as low as the men's if their pay was increased!

The type of labour in which women were found to be more valuable workers than men was light work of a repetitive nature, or work requiring special dexterity – often work classed as men's work before 1914. There were skilled processes which had been considered definitely and exclusively men's work before the war at which women became rapidly expert:

> In some skilled trades, such as acetylene welding, where the process, reserved before the war to fully-skilled fitters, boilermakers or coppersmiths, was more or less specialised, the women did 'interchange' jobs with the men and it was pretty generally accepted that woman's output is equal to the man's … in some cases it is said to be better. (Factory Inspectorate Report, 1920)

The medical officers working in industry noted the changes in women with their increased role in industry:

> Most women enjoyed the more interesting, active and arduous occupations, and in many cases their health improved rather than deteriorated. Medical officers

A man and a woman working together in the saw-milling industry. The lack of protection for the hands is deliberately recorded.

of factories and welfare supervisors have pointed out the beneficial effects of open-air conditions (yard work, trucking of raw materials etc.) on the general health, and the success with which properly selected women have undertaken work involving the lifting of weights, heavy machine work, and even forge and foundry work, without untoward physical consequences. The whole experience tends to show that light sedentary work is not by any means always the most suitable for women. That operations involving a change of posture are preferable and that given an adequate nutrition many women would have better health and greater physical vigour if they followed more active occupations … The conditions under which women were employed before the war were not such as to enable them to develop full health and vigour. Low wages, and unsatisfactory and inadequate diet, long hours and lack of exercise in the open air, resulted in physical and industrial inefficiency and caused both men and women to place too low a value upon the woman's strength and capacity. The results of employment of women under war conditions have emphasised the importance to health of good food, clothing and domestic comfort which can be obtained when the wages represent a reasonably adequate recompense for labour. They have also proved that properly nourished women have a much greater reserve of energy than they usually had been credited with and that under suitable conditions they can properly and advantageously be employed upon more occupations than has been considered desirable in the past even when these involve considerable activity, physical strain, exposure to weather etc. Light sedentary occupations are not necessarily healthy occupations. (War Cabinet Committee on Women in Industry, 1919)

The conclusions of the War Cabinet Committee on Women in Industry (1919) were that before the war, women had been paid such low wages they could not feed or support themselves properly; this had set up a vicious circle of low wages, low efficiency and low valuation of their work. Examining the effects of employment in industry and the health of women and their children, the War Cabinet Committee came to the following conclusion: 'Employment under suitable conditions is not itself injurious to the pregnant woman, while the money thus earned may enable her to be properly fed, a matter of the highest importance.'

During the wartime period there were lower infant mortality rates, while an increasing number of mothers were being employed in industry. Clearly irritated by the persistent search for differences between men's and women's ability to carry out industrial occupations Dr Butler, the medical officer of the Scottish Shell Filling Factory at Paisley, told the War Cabinet Committee:

There has been a tendency to exaggerate the physiological differences between men and women which is mainly connected with women's maternity function. Generally speaking the health of women who had worked indoors – domestic service etc., improved considerably with good food and physical work … there is no industrial work as heavy as charing and women should not be prevented from doing any work they are fit for, including foundry work, heavy engineering and heavy chemical work.

The report of the 1919 War Cabinet Committee assessed the contribution of women to the war effort and examined the future role of women in industry. The committee collected a wide range of evidence relating to women's work, both before and during the war. However, in producing its findings and recommendations, the committee was constrained by two fundamental assumptions: that men had a prior right to paid employment, and that the performance of domestic tasks was a function inseparable from womanhood. The committee recommended that a national minimum wage for women should be laid down by law, based upon the subsistence needs of a single woman; a pensions scheme was also advocated for women who had to support children without the aid of a man. The committee unanimously agreed that:

No woman should be employed for less than a reasonable subsistence wage – that this wage should be sufficient to provide a single woman over eighteen years of age in a typical district where the cost of living is low, with an adequate diet, with lodging to include fuel and light in a respectable house not more than half an hour's journey, including tram or train from the place of work, with clothing sufficient for warmth, cleanliness and decent appearance, with money for fares, insurance, Trade Union Subscription and with a reasonable sum for holidays and amusements.

The effect of these proposals was practically nil; no legislative provision was made for a national wage for women, and widows received a pension seven years after the proposals were made. Only Beatrice Webb, a member of the committee, raised a voice in opposition to the report, attacking the assumption 'that industry is normally a function of the male, and that women ... are only permitted to work for wages under special conditions.' Beatrice Webb's proposals in 1919, arising out of the experience of women working in industry during the period of World War One, are of great significance, particularly when one considers how relatively recently some of her proposals have been encompassed in legislation. Her five main proposals were:

Fixing the nose clips to gas masks, Holloway Road, London.

Work more traditionally associated with the nineteenth-century 'sweated trades': girls finishing teddy bears in a toy factory, Nell Foy, Church Street, Chelsea, 1918. The war led to the relaxation of the Factory Acts, with children as young as 12 working up to thirty-three hours a week. Photographer: G.P. Lewis.

i)   That there should be a national minimum wage, which should be equal for men and women.

ii) That there should be standard rates of remuneration for every occupation, which should be equal for men and women.

iii) That the principle of the 'vested interest' or prior right of the male to any occupation should be rejected.

iv) That provision should be made for children by the State.

v)   That adult dependants (such as aged, infirm and sick) should be also provided for as a national obligation, 'because it is not desirable that one adult should be dependent upon another adult for maintenance.'
(Report of War Cabinet Committee, Minority Report, 1919)

Reviewing the year following the end of the war, R.E. Graves, the Chief Inspector of Factories, felt that British industry had adjusted well to peacetime production and accommodating the demobilised men:

The first year after the cessation of hostilities has been a very notable one for industry, and it is remarkable how complete has been the change over from war to civil production, and with what wonderful smoothness this stupendous task has been accomplished on the whole. The first great step in the transformation was the gradual, and now almost complete, withdrawal of women from the men's industries where they performed such magnificent service during the War, and the absorption into industry of the demobilised men. (Women's Inspectorate Report, 1919)

One of the Lady Factory Inspectors added:

The change back has been effected with far less effort than was the earlier change from civil to war production, and this is largely an effect of the careful substitution agreements of employers and workers made in so many industries under the guidance of the Factory Department. (1919)

The difficulty for many men and women was that, while acknowledging that the enormous expansion in the size of the women's workforce had led to far-reaching economic and social changes, it was not easy to uphold the rights of both men and women to employment and equality of pay. The president of the Women's Labour League Congress in 1917 spelt out the dilemma facing women when the men returned from the front:

After the war ... was the woman going back like Joan of Arc to her plough and rough menial work? After delivering her country and laying down her armour was she going to leave the arena of commerce to lay down her uniform and go back to her pots and kettles, to unpaid and unconsidered labour or to the lower alleys of factory work?

Certainly the women themselves wished to remain in employment; in answer to the question posed in 1916, 'Do you wish after the war to return to your former work or stay in what you are doing now?', of the 3,000 answers, 2,500 were 'To stay in the work I am doing now.' It was clear that women did not want to return to the traditional and ill-paid jobs of the pre-war period. During their wartime employment women had gained substantially by achieving regular, well-paid employment, which allowed them and their families a higher standard of nutrition and health. However, even more important than their increased spending power was their greater freedom and importance in society and their acknowledged role within it. This feeling of a greater role within society was summarised in a letter to the *Glasgow Herald* in 1916:

A young woman operating a bottoming and flattening machine in a glass factory, Birmingham, 1918. The glass dust would have been inhaled by the worker. The installation of extraction fans was promoted by the Factory Inspectorate. Photographer: G.P. Lewis.

To observe how men speak and write about women today is vastly amusing to us. We have not changed with the war; it is only that in some instances the scales have fallen from men's eyes … In the hour of Britain's need her sons have realised that if victory was to be won they could not afford to hem in women with the old restrictions. To carry on the industries of the country women must work … A few years ago I heard Lord Charles Beresford say 'A woman's place was her home'. Twelve months ago I heard him say 'Woman's place was in the world'.

In spite of wishing to remain in their wartime industries, the demobilisation of troops forced women out of their jobs and back into their 'traditional pre-war areas of work' with their associated low pay and poor conditions. The pressure on women to leave their wartime jobs was enormous; campaigns were run in the press to 'persuade' women where their work lay:

> Women still have not brought themselves to realise that factory work, with the money paid for it during the war, will not be possible again ... Women who left domestic service to enter the factory are now required to return to the pots and pans. (*Southampton Times*, 1919)

Photographs from
the Women's War Work Committee

Milling grenades, Castlelaurie Foundry, Falkirk Iron Company.

WOMEN'S WELFARE AND WORKING CONDITIONS

Throughout the period of the war, considerable concern was expressed by organisations concerned with the welfare of women about the effects of 800,000 women entering industrial employment. The Women's Factory Inspectorate paid particular attention to the ability or inability of previously male-dominated industries to adapt to the employment of large numbers of women. Details were noted on the provision of medical and dental care, cloakroom arrangements, baths and washing arrangements, the provision of overalls, waterproofs, gloves etc., workroom cleanliness, seating accommodation and messroom arrangements.

In many industries men and women were working together for the first time; concern was expressed over the safety of the women, with night work raising particular difficulties. In general, unmarried women were not normally encouraged to carry out night-shift work. In most factories night-shift work was carried out under the supervision of a female supervisor and in ammunition factories a nurse was on duty should tiredness result in fainting. Women factory inspectors urged the provision of a good meal during the night shift. In some factories the organisation of meal breaks could be complicated; at one factory women were escorted to and from the dining-room, and when the women's shift left the factory a police patrol was on duty. Where the women workers could not be segregated from male workers, concern was frequently expressed:

In Birmingham factories the manufacture does not lend itself to a division between men's and women's work or to the employment of girls under a forewoman. Men and girls work side by side in big sheds filled by machinery. The sheds are situated in large yards which often at night are insufficiently lighted, and undoubtedly the women workers are exposed to serious risk. (Factory Inspectorate Report, 1917)

At the outbreak of the war, the majority of factories and workshops lacked any proper provision of messrooms or canteens; a survey in Sheffield at the start of the war showed that only 30 per cent of the factories provided simple dining rooms or areas where the workforce could eat their food. The introduction of night shifts for women, together with many women's difficulty obtaining food during the day due to rationing, led to improved conditions for canteens and messrooms; the Home Office, in granting orders for night work, expressly laid down the condition that suitable provision had to be made for messroom facilities. In many cases dining rooms and small kitchens were built; most new factories had facilities where workers could heat and eat a meal away from the factory floor. A woman inspector commenting upon the need for adequate catering noted:

> How greatly the army of industrial workers need a commissariat department to cater for them during their days of active service will perhaps be better realised now that the public attention has been riveted on the victualling of our soldiers in camp and at the front. If 'an army fights on its stomach' is it not also true that a factory works on it? On the one hand the workers require the opportunity to buy good nourishing food and to eat it under good conditions, on the other the money to spend on a sufficient dinner – to illustrate these needs the following out of numerous examples are given. A large factory has since the war been filled to its utmost capacity, working long hours on uniforms – at a dinner hour visit I found in every room on six floors, 12 rooms in all, the workers were seated at their work-tables and sewing machines eating their mid-day meal. The stuffy rooms were for the time a restaurant, the smell of cooked vegetables and fish being added to the general smell of humanity and cloth. The manager was much concerned, and asked if nothing could be done; he said he had spoken about it to his Directors till he was tired and there was no available room for a mess-room, and the restaurants and eating-houses in the neighbourhood were overfull in the dinner hour already. The workers were making good wages on War Office contracts, the Factory Act secured them the hour's break, they were hungry, the Army needed all the work these girls could turn out at top speed, but for lack of opportunity unsuitable and insufficient food was eaten under the very worst conditions. Referring to the second point, that sufficient money to spend on food is required, is illustrated by the fact that at a large East End restaurant where the mid-day meal is served daily to a hundred workers from a neighbouring factory the Superintendent and her helpers had for years deplored the insufficiency of the dinner purchased by the young girls under 16. Meat and vegetables were purchased by the elder girls and women, but a little pudding and gravy or tea and bread and butter was all the younger ones could afford. The ladies felt that these needed it as much as

their elders, and could scarcely refrain from supplying more than was paid for. One day soon after war broke out there was such a run on meat and vegetable dinners that the supply was not equal that day to the demand – all the young girls were asking to be served with them. The cause was that the wages had that day been raised voluntarily by the occupier to the proposed Trade Board rate, and the effect was immediate, and has continued. This fact is a striking answer to those who cling to the theory that an increase in wages is of no substantial value to a girl. (Annual Report, 1916)

In an attempt to encourage their workforce to take part in outdoor activities when away from the workplace, some firms provided allotments, sports fields and activity rooms. When the Women's Factory Inspectorate came across such provision they often described them with a sense of amazement:

Two firms have erected large buildings: they have billiard rooms, smoking rooms, rest rooms and restaurants all under the same roof. Clubs for sports as well as gardening; dramatic societies are organised and special teachers are appointed to teach gymnasium. A firm in the country near Bristol provides a certain number of allotments on which the workpeople can grow their own vegetables etc. This cannot be done in London, but one firm in the East have done their best to encourage workers who are keen on gardening and they have a club which provides seeds and gives information as to the best way of growing different plants, and award prizes for the best results that can be obtained in the East End backyards and window-boxes.

I saw a novelty in swimming baths at one factory where the entire roof is covered with two water tanks, one for boys and one for girls.

Despite such improvements, the inspectors came across frequent instances of the most appalling working conditions for women. Adequate sanitation was frequently a problem:

In the potteries where, in the past, considerable effort was made to get the local authorities of the Five Towns to give this matter their attention, great strides have been made during last year in altering and re-building sanitary accommodation. We have sent to the County Borough of Stoke over 100 notices of insufficient, insanitary or unsuitable accommodation for women. The Chief Inspector of Nuisances has kindly sent me a return of the work done during the year in his Borough, which shows that out of 1,413 defects found 1,294 have been remedied. Miss Whitlock reports that foul smelling privies are still met with and sometimes the number of conveniences is very inadequate, e.g., one convenience was found in one case for over 70 women. A small charge to workers for the cleaning of closets is fairly common, but the general standard of cleanliness in these places is not high. Miss Escreet found better conditions in Leicestershire than those to which she was accustomed in Lancashire but considers the metal trades and brick works of Staffordshire behind even the low standard of Lancashire.

In one town notices had to be sent in the case of 36 factories out of the 54 visited, and represented elementary defects in sanitation and suitability. Several bad cases have not yet been remedied though the original visits were paid in April and May.

Accommodation in brick yards is of the poorest. Notices of instruction to firms were sent in respect of 17 of the 22 works visited and further attention will be given to the matter in the current year. As the industry is a country one, the conveniences are privies, and careful scavenging arrangements should be made: these are frequently badly neglected. The women's and men's conveniences often stand doorless or unscreened side by side in a deserted portion of the yard, being totally unprovided with artificial light. It is amazing that such conditions should have been allowed to persist so long.

The problems of ventilation, excessive temperatures and poor lighting exercised the factory inspectors considerably. The textile and clothing industries, together with the laundry industry, raised particular problems in these areas:

In the large clothing factories, where power is readily available, the need for a more efficient and scientific system of ventilation remains obvious. Some occupiers still appear to have a rooted belief that a really good sized fan, revolving at the rate of many hundred revolutions a minute is a panacea for all the evils in connection with the vitiated air of factories. Repeatedly an occupier has taken us to see his fan, and has asked us to watch its revolutions and to calculate for ourselves the number of cubic feet of air and the number of microbes which the fan is hustling out of the factory each moment of the working day, and then it has been necessary to point out that the fan is so placed that it only creates a 'short circuit' and a draught in its own immediate neighbourhood. I hope that by the continued taking of air samples we may create a radical change in the present often defective installations. In some of the large factory laundries the need of more efficient means of ventilation, and of reduction of temperature raised by the steam and gas-heated machines is still pronounced. A factory which may be recorded as regular at one visit may, on another occasion, be far from healthy owing to atmospheric conditions. As Miss Ahrons points out, the ventilation of the town laundry is a difficult matter. Surrounded on all sides by factories and buildings with chimneys emitting smoke and dirt and filling the air with impurities, the windows and ventilators are often shut to prevent the smuts falling on the work. The occupiers complain that the fans draw the dust in through the various openings, so not only does the close proximity of the buildings shut out the fresh air, but the available means of ventilation are not sufficiently used. In one very enclosed laundry a propulsion system of ventilation by means of fans and ducts had recently been installed, but these ducts were laid near the floor, and the ventilating openings were covered with wire screens to prevent the entrance of dust and dirt. Although expense had been incurred by the installation of this plant very little benefit so far seemed to have been derived.

With women replacing men in many industries which involved labouring, particular concern was expressed regarding the work's effects on the physical health of the women. Before the war, women were involved in industries which required them to lift very considerable weights:

Owing to a complaint from a mother employed at an aerated water works that she considered the heavy work of lifting and carrying done by the women had been the cause of the still-birth of her baby, I made some enquiry in one factory. (a) Crates of twelve empty syphons weigh 68lbs.: they are lifted by a woman washer from the buffer's wheel to the washing machines. (b) A crate of 28 empty bottles (pint size) weight 42lbs.: such crates are lifted from the stack of cases of empty bottles a few feet off by a girl of 17 to the washing tank. (c) A crate of two dozen 10oz. crown lemonade bottles weights 56lbs.: such crates are lifted by a woman from the bottling machines to the labeller's bench.

Also owing to a complaint as to the heavy nature of her employment, received from a young mother employed in a brick works, whose baby had died almost immediately after birth, and who returned to the factory within a month of her confinement, I visited the brick works at which she had been employed. I found that the women fill and empty the stoves in which the bricks are fired, that they take off at the making machine, also riddle and build up the bricks in the yard. Two women and two men form an emptying squad, the women being employed only in the kiln, while the man wheels away the brick laden bogie. A filling squad is composed of two women and one man, the man wheeling the bricks from the making machine, while the women build up the bricks. The weight of the largest brick is about 81/4lbs. The women lift two of these bricks simultaneously, one in each hand, both in filling and in emptying the kilns, and as the total number of bricks made averages 13,000 a day, each woman lifts about 6,500, i.e., over 52,000lbs. or 464cwt. The temperature in the warmest part of one of the kilns at a point at which the women were emptying, I found to be from 103°F., the outside temperature being 48°. (Annual Report, 1917)

Following the war an assessment of women's ability to undertake heavy manual labour was carried out by a number of employers' federations; in general they found that one man's work might be replaced by 1.6 to 2.8 of a woman's, although with the introduction of labour-saving devices this ratio was considerably reduced in some industries.

In organising the work of the two photographers, Nicholls and Lewis, the Women's Factory Inspectorate clearly used their local inspectors to brief the photographers on the industrial processes to be recorded and the details – such as the positioning of the hands near dangerous machinery, clothing, safety garments worn, etc – which they wanted recorded. These photographs were later incorporated into the department's library of 'good and bad practice'.

One woman could vividly recall the terrible conditions she worked in after more than fifty years:

The outside of this grim establishment looked dark and dirty, the windows in the compressed leather department were boarded half way up, this I presume was to stop vandalism but it did nothing to improve the dark, damp smelly interior where about forty young girls and women toiled for ten hours every day clad in thick heavy shoes and a large heavy leather apron to protect their clothing which, by the way failed miserably, for one could not fail to correct some of the evil smelling concoction you worked with, from attaching itself to your blouse. It was a huge place, one side having heavy long tables at which each girl was allocated about four feet of working space, standing in close proximity of each other, but never daring to speak for fear you would hear your number called out, with the order to go home for the day and the words 'you have come here to work not to a party'. Despite this there were moments when the overlooker would leave her point of vantage and some daring mortal would burst into song, tho God knows what any of us had to sing about in these conditions.

The main heavy gates opened into a kind of archway and it was from this point the gatekeeper rang his bell, this being up in the belfry on the top of the buildings. It was rung every morning to signal us both in and out, if you were two minutes late after the clanging, which could be heard quite a considerable distance away, you were fined three checks or the equivalent of three pennies.

This we could ill afford, and should the dreaded sound occur before we were near the gate we would run as fast as our legs could carry us to try to defeat its dreaded purpose. Once through the portals you were safe for the gatekeeper must lock them, this was one of his tasks. There was a glass-top-roof lean-to building which served as a cloakroom, dining room, at one end stood an old iron gas stove, no oven just open jets on the top which when covered with an iron plate was used for hotting the dinners we carried in our baskets from home, in a basin of course. For frying there was one iron frying pan which we took in turns to use as the occasion arose. We also took it in turns to light the stove and on Friday, after dinner, scrub the wooden tables we ate off, very rarely was the floor touched except for a quick sweeping and the walls of the place were festooned with spiders' webs, so much for the dining room. The toilets where intricacies I never did understand for they were only flushed about once a day by some unseen method. These also we took turns to clean, for the washing of our hands there was a huge tank filled from the River Leen whose waters were used in the process of tanning, no towel or even rag to dry them on, no such luxury. (Nottingham tannery worker, 1917)

A woman operating a sand-blasting machine on a memorial stone decorated with a Celtic cross – the mask does not have a protective filter against breathing in the dust. Instead, the worker is wearing what was effectively a rubber bag over her head, which must have been extremely unpleasant. The stone particles produced by the blasting can be seen on the glass of her protective goggles. Messrs Stewart & Co. Ltd, Fraser Place, Aberdeen, Scotland, September 1918. Photographer: G.P. Lewis.

Sewing asbestos mattresses by hand for lining ships' boilers, Messrs Turner Brothers Asbestos Factory, Trafford Park, Manchester, September 1918. The dangers of asbestos were not known at the time, although women who worked with the material were known to suffer from 'asbestos throat'. Photographer: G.P. Lewis.

Sheet of glass being carried out of the warehouse, Lancashire glass works, 1918. Note the lack of protection for the hands. Photographer: G.P. Lewis.

An outdoor labourer working in a paper mill, Scotland, October 1918. Photographer: G.P. Lewis.

An example of a clean, modern canteen room for munitions workers, 1918.

An exemplary factory canteen dining room, 1918.

Small messroom for textile workers. Note the segregation from men and the presence of a woman supervisor.

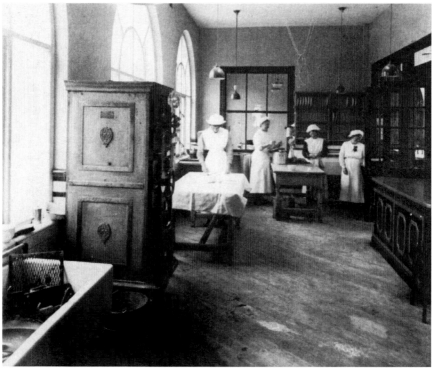

Above: A large group of female millers smile for the camera outside a Lancashire flour mill, 1918. In the background, the mill building is visible, as are some male mill workers. Photographer: G.P. Lewis.

Opposite top: Modern canteen kitchen with warming stove to the fore and gas oven on the right. The provision of food in the government factories led to an improvement in women's diet and health. (1918)

Opposite bottom: A simple restroom for foundry workers to rest in and eat their own food. 'First of all we worked full time from six o'clock in the morning till five at night, and from five at night till six in the morning and that was the nights … as they got more girls in, they thought they would get more work out and they worked it at eight hours … that was, six to two, and two till ten and ten till six in the morning and that was the three shifts.' (Foundry worker 1918)

A female worker rolls a barrel of beer into a storage house at a Stafford brewery, September 1918. Photographer: G.P. Lewis

First-aid room in a munitions factory.

Restroom in a small factory.

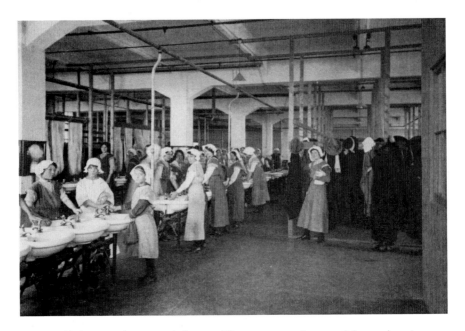

Washing facilities in a large textile factory. The young age of some of the workers is notable.

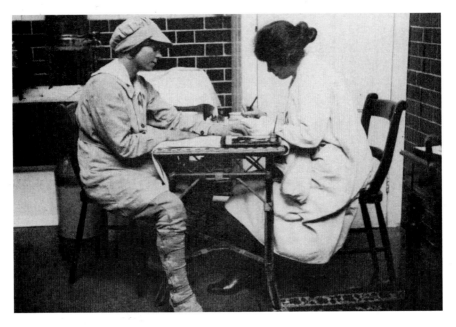

Woman doctor running a surgery for munitions workers, 1918. 'She hadn't a hat on and of course it was a drilling machine. They're easy enough to them drilling machines; you just drill a hole for the screw. Anyway she just happened to turn her head and her hair was loose and caught her hair in it. The screams, it was terrible, I remember it now.' (Engineering factory worker, oral history)

Simple bathroom in a factory. This would have been regarded as being rare in this period.

Gymnasium for women.

Athletics ground for textile workers.

Allotment for factory workers.

Metal Industries, Munitions and Other War Work

In the metal industries before World War One women were employed in tin-plate manufacture and wire drawing, as well as in the making of chains, nails, bolts, screws, rivets, etc. They were also employed in the production of light castings and allied trades (tinned and japanned goods). In the tin-plate industries they were employed in pickling and preparing the plates for the tin bath. In chain-making they made the smaller hand-hammered chains used mainly for agricultural purposes. Women fed the nail-cutting and tack machines, working in the Black Country and Birmingham on light machines for turning, screwing and pointing bolts, and for facing and topping nuts. Women were also employed in the warehouses, packing and bagging all these articles. Before World War One the machines were all set by male tool setters.

In general engineering women were employed before World War One mainly in specialised factories in the Midlands on repetition work. They worked on capstan lathes, power hand presses, stamping, drilling, plating and hand soldering. The machines for the production of several components for small-arms ammunition in Birmingham and Newcastle were worked by women, although this was unusual for the period.

During World War One, it was first and foremost requirements for munitions which brought women into the metal trades. Up to December 1914, only 3,000 women had entered the industry. Over the following six months the shortage of munitions became increasingly acute. Initially, attempts were made to increase production using the existing male workforce by improving production techniques; women were gradually introduced during this period but were restricted to the unskilled processes. By the second half of 1915, the failure of the munitions industry to meet the demands of the war led to another 45,000 women being absorbed by the industry and the dilution process began in earnest, with women replacing men in many areas of production. Between July 1914 and

July 1918 the numbers of women employed in the metal industries rose from 170 000 to 594,000, 90 per cent of whom performed work customarily performed by men. To the 424,000 women who entered the industry an additional 223,000 should be added, as these were the women who worked in national establishments producing munitions, most of whom worked on metal. Unsurprisingly, the most important area of activity was shell making. By the middle of the war, women formed 60 per cent of the workforce producing shells and were involved with all aspects of shell making, from the roughing and turning of the bodies to the final gauging of the completed shell.

> [My first job was] filling 9:2 gas shells … and they started us first on stemming the shells there was a certain amount of the powder measured out to you and you had to start on the shell from the bottom to the top and the stem was just like the handle of a brush, and of course you had a wooden mallet and then you had to start and hammer from the bottom to the top because you had to get it all in and if you didn't there was too much left over … I was promoted from stemming shells to a press operator and of course we weren't allowed to wear any of our clothes, we had to strip out. If you had linen buttons on there was tin inside, you see and it would cause an explosion … we were supplied with cocoa going on duty and coming off and we had our own surgery and doctor … The nurse examined you, they could tell by the colour of our eyes whether the gas was affecting us many way. Your hair didn't go yellow but when you went to bed as you took your head off the pillow the pillowslip was pink. (Munitions worker in a gas shell factory)

In general engineering shops, shipyards, aircraft factories, etc., women were introduced to most varieties of men's work – light engineering, turning, shaping, machine riveting, crane-driving, soldering, welding; some women were promoted to the normally protected male areas of responsibility for fitting and turners. This process of introducing women to the engineering workshop was to greatly hasten the pre-war movement for specialisation on the shop-floor and the subdivision of processes.

At the end of the war the National Employers' Federation submitted an assessment of the performance of women working in the engineering and metal industries in comparison with men. With regard to output, it concluded:

I. Quality:

Sheet metal – Women's work better than men's output.
Engineering – Women's output equal to that of boys.
Repetitive light work – Women equal to men and boys.

Aircraft woodwork – Women equal to men in most areas.
Cartridge production – Women equal to men.
Shell production – Women's work poorer than men's.

2. Quantity:

Sheet metal – Women's production equal to 99 per cent of men's output.
Engineering – Women's production equal to 75 per cent of men's output.
Repetitive light work – Women's production equal to men's output.
Aircraft woodwork – Women's production equal to men's output.
Cartridge production – Women's production equal to men's output, in some cases 20 per cent more than men's.
Shell production – Women's production behind that of men and boys.

For labouring tasks three women were considered as being equivalent to two men and generally the Employers' Federation placed women's wartime production as being two-thirds of men's in value. Overall, women equalled and sometimes surpassed men's work, but could not compete due to lack of training or physical reasons – it was found that for light repetitive work women were both more efficient and productive. Some employers suggested that women's production involved more waste. However, a major employer in the Midlands running six shell-making factories testified to the waste produced by women as being 'infinitesimally low'.

Women were prohibited from being involved in the actual processes of smelting throughout the war, but women performed the same work as boys in cold-rolling, and to some extent in pickling and opening tin plates – a heavy operation. In many factories women were employed as unskilled labourers performing heavy labouring duties and as crane-drivers.

They took me up, showed me the controls – after a couple of days you got used to it … you had to come down every hour and a half to drink milk to get rid of the effects of the fumes. You drank half a pint of milk to clear the fumes. (Female crane operator, Southampton Oral History Archive)

Woman tin plate worker feeding the cold rolling machine at the Beaufort Tin Plate Works, Maureston, South Wales, 1918. Photographer: G.P. Lewis.

Tin plates about to be dipped into pickling baths at the Beaufort Tin Plate Works, Maureston, South Wales, 1918. Photographer: G.P. Lewis.

Women trucking tin plates from the pickling room at the Beaufort Tin Plate Works, Maureston, South Wales, 1918. Photographer: G.P. Lewis.

Woman tin plate worker removing the tin plates from the annealing stand at Beaufort Tin Plate Works Maureston, South Wales, 1918. Many women's hair turned white from the acid fumes. Photographer: G.P. Lewis.

Tin plates being separated, Beaufort Tin Plate Works, Maureston, South Wales, 1918. The work-bench is placed by the window to make the best use of natural light. Photographer: G.P. Lewis.

Women munitions workers operating a circular saw to cut a steel bar in the production of shells, possibly at the National Projectile Factory, 1918. The lack of protective clothing or machine guards is notable.

Women steel workers handling the hot slag heads into which the waste slag is poured, National Projectile Factory, 1918.

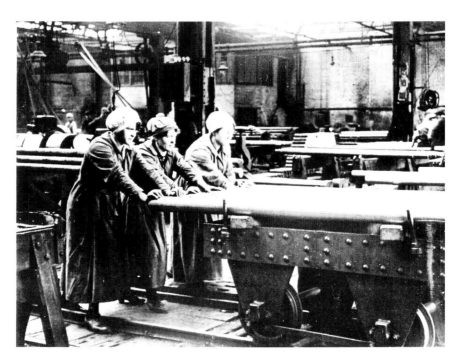

Women trucking steel bars. National Projectile Factory, 1918.

Six-inch chemical shells being cleaned, Falkirk Iron Company, Castlelaurie Foundry, 1917.

Women carrying 6-inch chemical shell cores, Falkirk Iron Company, Castlelaurie Foundry, 1917.

Women labourers emptying the ash wagons from the steelworks, National Projectile Factory, 1918.

The inspection room of the foundry where the steel bars were inspected for quality, National Projectile Factory, 1918.

Women operating lathes in the production of steel rails, David Brown & Sons, Sheffield, 1918.

Women operating punching machine in foundry to produce 'fish plates' for the railways, David Brown & Sons, Sheffield, 1918.

Woman crane driver moving a load of steel rails, David Brown & Sons, Sheffield, 1918.

Women milling the calibration sections for range-finding equipment, Barr and Stroud, Glasgow, 1918.

Women engraving and dividing the scales on range-finders for the navy and army, Barr and Stroud, Glasgow, 1918.

Women assembling the instrumentation for naval fire-control systems, Barr and Stroud, Glasgow, 1918.

Making the rubber mouth pieces for the gas masks using moulds, Crowndale Works, Camden Town, London, 1918. Photographer: G.P. Lewis.

Cleaning and examining the glasses for eyepieces in gas masks, Crowndale Works, Camden Town, London, 1918. Photographer: G.P. Lewis.

The oven room for producing splinterless glass for gas masks, Crowndale Works, Camden Town, London, 1918. Photographer: G.P. Lewis.

A female worker places pieces of glass used in gas masks into an oven to harden the dope at the Crowndale Works, Camden Town, London, 1918. Photographer: G.P. Lewis.

The doping room at the Crowndale Works, where the canvas masks were sealed against gas, Camden Town, London, 1918. Photographer: G.P. Lewis.

Detail of the doping process for gas masks, Crowndale Works, Camden Town, London, 1918. Photographer: G.P. Lewis.

Sewing nose clips for gas masks, unknown factory in Holloway Road, London, 1918.

The packing room for gas masks, unknown factory in Holloway Road, London, 1918.

WOOD AND AIRCRAFT TRADES

During World War One the proportion of women employed in the wood and aircraft trades increased from 15 per cent to over 33 per cent of the total workforce.

Women were involved in wood-milling, sawing, planing, assembly, painting, polishing, varnishing, doping and metalwork. The workforce increased by 35,000 women, 23,000 of whom directly replaced men. A few thousand of these went into saw-milling but the turnover was high, as the work was extremely heavy and required long training. The most important area was aircraft manufacture; at the outbreak of the war the industry was still in the experimental stage, employing a small workforce of skilled mechanics and woodworkers such as cabinet-makers. By the end of the war the industry was composed of a series of subdivided processes where over a third of the workforce was female. By the end of 1918, 55,000 aircraft had been produced.

Women were involved in the cutting and sawing of the linen fabric for the fuselage and wings, as well as painting on the acetate dope and assembling the aircraft. There was much resistance to the employment of women in any areas involving woodcutting and woodworking by the National Amalgamated Furnishing Trades Association. A circular issued by the Minister of Munitions in 1916, which urged employers to take on female labour in the aircraft industry, met with so much opposition that it had to be withdrawn. Subsequently the National Aircraft Committee laid down that 'women should not be permitted to use edge tools' or be employed 'on any wood-cutting processes connected with aircraft'. 'Substituted' women in aircraft woodworking were mainly employed in assembly work or in the cutting and sewing of linen fabric for the aircraft bodies.

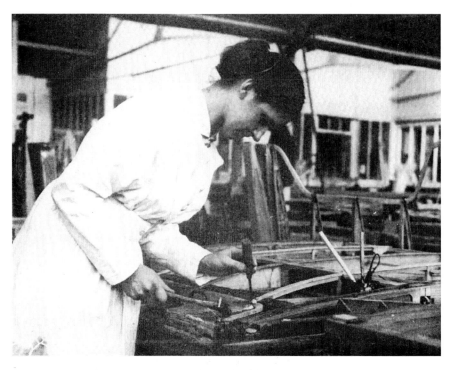

Woman aircraft worker constructing the centre portion of a frame for an aircraft wing. 'My brother was working on aeroplanes, they were up and coming then, so I thought, why can't a girl go down there? They are taking girls to work on the sewing part of the wings. They were covered in linen and then doped (moisture proofed). That was done in a loft. They employed about ten or twelve girls.' (Aircraft worker, Southampton)

Card splicing the joints on the frame of a wing for an aeroplane, Austin Motor Works, Northfield, near Birmingham, 1918. Photographer: G.P. Lewis.

Taping and preparing the frames of the wings of aeroplanes for the canvas covering, Austin Motor Works, Northfield, near Birmingham, 1918. Photographer: G.P. Lewis.

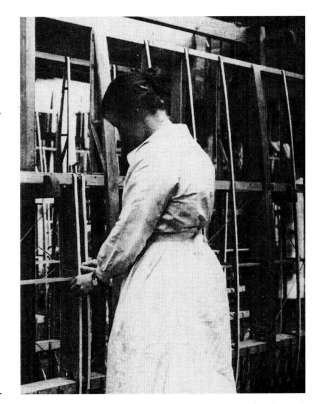

Women stitching the canvas on the fuselage covers, Austin Motor Works, Northfield, near Birmingham, 1918. Photographer: G.P. Lewis.

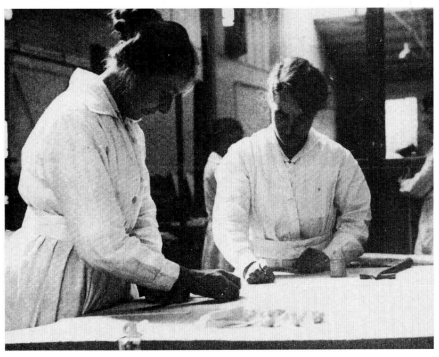

Women doping the wings of an aeroplane to strengthen and waterproof them, Austin Motor Works. Northfield, near Birmingham, 1918. The powerful fumes of the dope often caused breathing difficulties. Ventilation of the work areas was vital. Photographer: G.P. Lewis.

The national markings being painted on the wings of an aeroplane, Austin Motor Works. Northfield, near Birmingham, 1918. Photographer: G.P. Lewis.

Woman metal worker, acetylene welding frame lugs for plane assembly, Austin Motor Works. Northfield, near Birmingham, 1918. Photographer: G.P. Lewis.

Young girl operating the circular saw at N.G. Tarrant and Sons, Glasgow, 1918. Note the absence of protection for the face and hands.

Women 'trucking' the side pieces for the production of ammunition boxes, N.G. Tarrant and Sons, Glasgow, 1918.

Assembly of packing cases for ammunition, N.G. Tarrant and Sons, Glasgow, 1918. Before the war, carpentry was traditionally undertaken by men.

Woodworkers machine-wiring batches of side pieces for ammunition boxes, N.G. Tarrant and Sons, 1918.

CHINA AND EARTHENWARE TRADES

In 1914 two-fifths of the workforce were female in the china and earthenware industries, about 60 per cent of whom were employed in the Stoke-on-Trent district. Women were usually employed in departments on their own: working as decorators, aerographers, transferers, potters' attendants or dippers' helpers, as well as working as labourers in the yard and in the warehouse. In some areas of production women competed with men before the war: bowl-making, plate- and saucer-making and dipping. During the war the numbers of women increased by 10 per cent, with some 5,000 women directly replacing men.

Due to the dangers of lead poisoning, women involved with dipping or aerography were supposed to undergo a monthly medical throughout their period of war work. The women factory inspectors were alert to the dangers of lead poisoning, cases of which were reported before the war:

> Poverty, with its attendant worry and lack of nourishment, appeared to be a predisposing cause in many cases … in one case occurring in the first year of lead work, the patient had a gastric ulcer and in another case in the first year of lead work the patient had a stillborn child.

In these industries enormously heavy loads were carried by women. At the outbreak of war the inspectors found young women carrying wads of clay which weighed 48lb.

Worse cases were reported in the brickworks, where an inspector found:

> the temperature at floor level to be 120°, 112°, and 108°, and girls under 18 were employed in filling and pushing barrows of bricks, 50 bricks at a time, weighing 425lbs. In this case the weight was not so trying as it might be as the barrow was one of four wheels and therefore easy to push. In other places the barrow is on three wheels and the girls lift by the handles instead of pushing so that the burden is far greater even though the actual weight is less – 306lbs. Miss

Taylor says 'nine bricks weighing 8lbs., total over 60lbs., would be lifted as part of the work all day long'. The foreman at one of these works said to me, 'There is no work so hard as this throughout the country,' and I am sure he is right. (Factory Inspectorate Annual Report 1913)

Bricks being loaded onto railway wagons by female yard workers, Hathern station, Brick and Terra Cotta Company Ltd, Leicestershire, 1918.

Women yard workers feeding the machine for recovering silica stone, South Wales, 1918. Photographer: G.P. Lewis.

Women brickmakers trucking clay from the mills for silica brickmaking, South Wales, 1918. Photographer: G.P. Lewis.

Trucking clay to the moulding
house, South Wales, 1918.
Photographer: G.P. Lewis.

Woman brickworker filling
brick moulds with silica
clay, South Wales, 1918.
Photographer: G.P. Lewis.

Concrete bricks being
pressed into moulds.

Jubilant Welsh silica brickworkers, South Wales, 1918.

Women yard workers packing dried concrete bricks in railway wagons. The carrying of heavy weights by women was a persistent concern for the factory inspectors.

Woman yard worker emptying limestone slag from railway wagons.

Women barrowing limestone rocks at a cement works, Scotland, 1918. Photographer: G.P. Lewis.

Women clinker house workers at a cement works, Scotland, 1918. Photographer: G.P. Lewis.

Hoppers being filled with limestone, cement works, Scotland 1918. Photographer: G.P. Lewis.

Bagging cement, cement works, Scotland 1918. Photographer: G.P. Lewis.

The quality of cement being tested by a female chemist, cement works, Scotland 1918. Photographer: G.P. Lewis.

A granite block being positioned before being sawn by machine, Messrs Stewart & Co. Ltd, Fraser Place, Aberdeen, Scotland, September 1918. Photographer: G.P. Lewis.

A polishing machine being adjusted above a granite memorial stone, Messrs Stewart & Co. Ltd, Fraser Place, Aberdeen, Scotland, September 1918. Photographer: G.P. Lewis.

Woman worker, in a protective hood, sand-blasting a memorial stone, Messrs Stewart & Co. Ltd, Fraser Place, Aberdeen, Scotland, September 1918. Photographer: G.P. Lewis.

Women cleaning finished granite memorial stone, Messrs Stewart & Co. Ltd, Fraser Place, Aberdeen, Scotland, September 1918. Photographer: G.P. Lewis.

Draughtswoman working on the designs for memorial stones, Messrs Stewart & Co. Ltd, Fraser Place, Aberdeen, Scotland, September 1918. Photographer: G.P. Lewis.

Used moulds being
cleaned before re-use,
Stoke-on-Trent, 1918.

Fired taps being ground in poorly ventilated and lit conditions, Stoke-on-Trent, 1918.
Photographer: G.P. Lewis.

Fettling an absorption tower, Stoke-on-Trent, 1918. Photographer: G.P. Lewis.

The mouths to acid stoneware tanks being finished before inserting the taps, Stoke-on-Trent, 1918. Photographer: G.P. Lewis.

Preparing the plates for nitrating pans which were used in the manufacture of gun cotton, Terra Cotta Works, Leicestershire, 1918. Photographer: G.P. Lewis.

Moulding and finishing plates for nitrating pans, Terra Cotta Works, Leicestershire, 1918. Photographer: G.P. Lewis.

Group of terra cotta workers outside kiln, Leicestershire, 1918. Photographer: G.P. Lewis.

Clay heap workers piling up the raw clay for use in the pottery industry, Stoke-on-Trent, 1918. The clothing worn by the two women is unusual; it is possible that they are Land Army girls drafted in for the photograph.

Clay being fed into a mechanical tempering machine, Stoke-on-Trent, 1918.

Furnace workers feeding coke to the furnaces in order to fire the pottery kilns, Stoke-on-Trent, 1918.

Kiln workers loading a bottle kiln (the kiln on the right has been sealed with bricks before firing), Stoke-on-Trent, 1918.

Kiln worker removing the shattered pots after a firing, Stoke-on-Trent, 1918.

Oven being emptied mechanically.

Pottery being finished by grinding down rough areas on an abrasive wheel, Stoke-on-Trent, 1918.

Oven being emptied by hand, Stoke-on-Trent, 1918.

Washhouse workers in a Stoke-on-Trent pottery, 1918.

Packing area in a pottery.

Pottery medallions being moulded by hand.

Tiles being checked after firing.

Fine pottery being decorated by hand.

LEATHER TRADES

During the war the number of women in the leather trades increased from 23,100 in July 1914 to 43,000 in 1918, the overwhelming majority of whom directly replaced men. Few women were employed in the heavy leather-tanning industry before the war; they were largely confined to the dry operations in the warehouses. By 1918 a third of the workforce in the tanning industry was female. Women were employed in every area of work, both wet and dry, normally carrying out work which previously had been performed by youths. The Employers' Association at the end of the war assessed the performance of women, commenting on the high quality of their work, particularly in the areas requiring delicate handling and work which was of a repetitive nature. The employers noted that the women's timekeeping was better than the men's.

Some called it the compo shop, and others the knocking shop with a leering grin, the reason for this was that every girl was supplied with a large wooden mallet and a strong pair of scissors about ten to twelve inches long. These were her stock in trade without which she could not work, the mallets had an iron plate on the bottom and the shears were used to cut any thick skins.

The men started work at six a.m. and it was one of their tasks to wet the small skins, some of which were very small one never let your imagination run riot, this would be too horrible.

There was a huge vat filled with a boiling starchy liquid into which the bags of dried skins were emptied and allowed to pregnate for a period of time, they were then removed and drained on a huge slimey table from which they were weighed out. The girl would take the portion of slimey mess to her table on which was placed an iron frame, similar to a picture frame, measuring about twenty four inches by eighteen. There she would pick out the larger skins none of them more than four or five inches and stretch them on to the frame which stood on a hessian base. She would then proceed to fill in the centre of the frame with the pulpy mass left over, when this operation had been done she would take up the mallet and hammer the horrible mess until it was level and smooth, no holes left.

Then she would turn in the edges of the layer on the bottom, the ends having been left over the rim of the frame in order to make a seal. This done she would proceed to place the skins left over on to the top of the layer of hammered pulp, this must be a neat operation otherwise the work was spoiled. The she would dash to the press which stood on the other side of the room and take up a square flat tin the same size as the sheet of work she had made, return to her table and transfer the whole thing on to the tray, place her number on the work rush over to the overlooker who could, if she so decided tear up the whole construction, or send you back to your table to patch it up. If you were lucky you would reach the 'old gals; table, this name was a sort of endearment, before anyone was there, and be rewarded for your work by a check which was the equivalent of one penny. These you stored in a tin and every morning at eleven a.m. you would join the queue to hand them into the office where the 'Old man' sat waiting. He entered the number of these checks into the book and the more you handed him the larger your pay on Friday evening. (Woman leather worker, 1917)

Women tannery workers operating a 'setting out' machine, Nottingham, 1918.

Young tan-yard workers at the Pavlova Leather Company, Abingdon, 1918. The replacement of men by women in the tanning trade saw the percentage of women in the industry rising from 9 per cent to 38 per cent.

CHEMICAL INDUSTRIES

Before World War One there were four times as many men as women employed in the fine chemical and drug industries, and very few women worked in the heavy chemical industries. In all branches of the industry women were chiefly employed in the filling, labelling and finishing of packets or jars of chemicals or in the sorting and cleaning of bottles and jars. No women were employed in the Royal Gunpowder Factory before the war; a few women were employed at private explosive factories, mainly in the areas of teasing cotton, paste mixing for cordite, weighing and blending of cordite and making of blasting cartridges.

During the war the proportion of women working in the chemical industry rose from 20 per cent of the workforce to 39 per cent; the numbers of women increased by 64,000, some 34,000 of whom directly replaced men. The production of explosives absorbed the majority of these women, but the soap and candle industries also took in large numbers, in an area where women had not previously worked in significant numbers. In the heavy chemical industries, women were introduced during the war mainly as labourers, and were involved in packing, loading, unloading, trucking, wheeling and otherwise moving materials, and in general yard work. Depending upon the nature of the work, the Chemical Employers' Federation indicated that they considered between 1.6 and 2.8 women were required to replace one man.

The Employers' Federation suggested that they were incurring additional costs by having to provide welfare supervisors, canteens, bath attendants, nurses, canteen staff, etc. for their female employees, and these costs after the war would discourage them from employing large numbers of women.

The cork shed where the raw cork was stored in bales at the linoleum works of Messrs Barry Ostlere and Shepherd Ltd, Kirkcaldy, Fife, August 1918. Photographer: G.P. Lewis.

Cork-breaking area where the cork was ground at the linoleum works of Messrs Barry Ostlere and Shepherd Ltd, Kirkcaldy, Fife, August 1918. Photographer: G.P. Lewis.

The printing and coating machines for printing the designs on to the surface of the cork at the linoleum works of Messrs Barry Ostlere and Shepherd Ltd, Kirkcaldy, Fife, August 1918. Photographer: G.P. Lewis.

The packing floor at the linoleum works of Messrs Barry Ostlere and Shepherd Ltd, Kirkcaldy, Fife, August 1918. Photographer: G.P. Lewis.

Examining tables in the hand-finishing shop at the linoleum works of Messrs Barry Ostlere and Shepherd Ltd, Kirkcaldy, Fife, August 1918. Photographer: G.P. Lewis.

Dust abstractor plant for removing dust from the asbestos fibre, Turner Brothers, Trafford Park, Manchester, 1918.

Wheeling a bogey with wet asbestos millboard sheets to the drying room, Turner Brothers, Manchester, 1918.

Dried asbestos sheeting being stacked, Turner Brothers, Manchester, 1918.

Wet asbestos sheets being moulded into shape to form roofing sheets, Turner Brothers, Manchester, 1918.

Asbestos roofing sheets being loaded onto railway wagons, Turner Brothers, Manchester, 1918.

Corrugated asbestos sheeting being cut by a guillotine, Turner Brothers, Manchester, 1918.

Women workers sewing asbestos mattresses which were used for lining the boilers of the Royal Navy, Turner Brothers Asbestos Factory, September 1918. At the time of World War One asbestos was not recognised as the extreme health hazard which it is today. However, the dangers of working in industries involving high levels of dust were increasingly recorded by the factory inspectors. The women inspectors increasingly pressed for safer conditions through the introduction of dust extraction. Photographer: G.P. Lewis.

Asbestos mattresses being trucked to a warehouse, Turner Brothers, Manchester, 1918.

Asbestos cylinders for smoke shells being made by hand, Turner Brothers, Manchester, 1918.

The treads on a rubber tyre being built up by hand, Charles Makintosh and Sons Ltd, Manchester, September 1918. Photographer: G.P. Lewis.

Stripping and hoisting tyres on frames for removal before applying the tread, Charles Makintosh and Sons Ltd, Manchester, September 1918. Photographer: G.P. Lewis.

Hoisting a tyre on a pulley for removal to the press, Charles Makintosh and Sons Ltd, Manchester, September 1918. Photographer: G.P. Lewis.

Fixing studded tread to a tyre, Charles Makintosh and Sons Ltd, Manchester, September 1918. Photographer: G.P. Lewis.

Trucking the raw rubber
from the warehouse,
Wood-Milne, Leyland,
Lancashire.

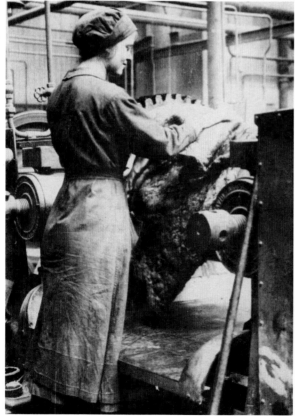

Raw rubber ring
being warmed up and
separated, Wood-Milne,
Leyland, Lancashire.

Raw rubber ring being warmed
on a mill.

Sheet rubber being prepared by being calendered, Wood-Milne, Leyland, Lancashire.

Warm rubber ring being carried to the spreading room, Wood-Milne, Leyland, Lancashire.

Woman rubber worker operating a spreading machine which coated canvas for tyre manufacture, Charles Mackintosh and Sons Ltd, Manchester, September 1918. Photographer: G.P. Lewis.

Rubber inner tubes being made by hand, Charles Mackintosh and Sons Ltd, Manchester, September 1918. Photographer: G.P. Lewis.

Rubber tubing being placed inside the vulcanisers, Charles Mackintosh and Sons Ltd, Manchester, September 1918. Photographer: G.P. Lewis.

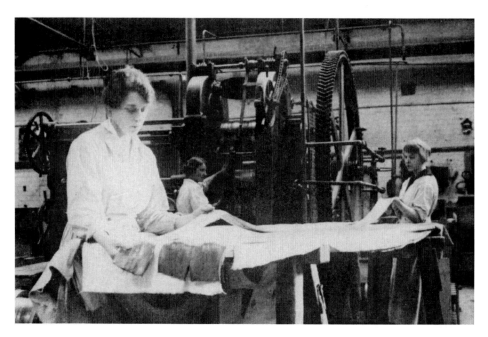

Calendering the rubber for producing a tread on a motor tyre, Charles Mackintosh and Sons Ltd, Manchester, September 1918. The tread was produced by running the soft rubber through the iron wheel in the background. Photographer: G.P. Lewis.

Women glass workers separating the cord from glass, Lancashire glass works, 1918. Note the poor protection for the hands when handling the razor-sharp raw glass pieces. Photographer: G.P. Lewis.

Women sludge-pit workers treating the residue from the sand washing tables of a Lancashire glass works, 1918. Photographer: G.P. Lewis.

Sand being prepared for grinding, Lancashire glass works, 1918. Photographer: G.P. Lewis.

Plaster house workers wearing protective masks. The plaster was used for bedding the glass on the surfacing tables, Lancashire glass works, 1918. Photographer: G.P. Lewis.

Trucking the glass composition to furnace pots before firing, Lancashire glass works, 1918. Photographer: G.P. Lewis.

Holding the glass in
position on the Lehr tables,
Lancashire glass works, 1918.
Photographer: G.P. Lewis.

Women removing the glass from the Lehr table under the supervision of a male foreman,
Lancashire glass works, 1918. Photographer: G.P. Lewis.

Glass being cleaned and inspected on a wooden 'horse', Lancashire glass works, 1918. Photographer: G.P. Lewis.

Women carrying a sheet of glass from the Lehr table, Lancashire glass works, 1918. Photographer: G.P. Lewis.

Women removing used emery 'fells' which were used in polishing plate glass, Lancashire, 1918. Photographer: G.P. Lewis.

Making wooden crates for rolled glass, Lancashire glass works, 1918. Photographer: G.P. Lewis.

Women operating glass-cutting machines with no protection for the face or hands.

Woman engraving a glass bowl.

Women grinding smooth the bottoms of glass measuring jugs.

Cutting off miners' lamp glasses.

Thick glass for submarine portholes being packed, Lancashire, 1918. Photographer: G.P. Lewis.

PAPER AND PRINTING TRADES

The principal paper and printing trades in which women were employed before the war were printing, bookbinding, cardboard-box and paper making and paper-bag manufacture. The trade unions prevented women from preparing the machines or 'making ready' any job, although they could take the sheets of paper from the letter press. In Scotland, women were allowed to be involved in composition in the printing trade to a limited degree. In bookbinding, especially in the less skilled areas, women were employed on various stages of production such as paging, collating, folding and sewing. During the war the percentage of the total workforce employed by the paper and printing industries composed of women rose from 36 per cent to 48 per cent, with 21,000 women directly replacing men. Married women were not discouraged from performing night work despite attempts by employers to relax the Factory and Workshop Acts, and replaced men mainly in warehouse work, bookbinding and paper making.

Warehouse where rags used in paper-making were sorted.

Women labourers feeding rags into the pulping machines, Scotland, October 1918. Photographer: G.P. Lewis.

Woman operating a machine for breaking up rags at a paper works in Scotland, October 1918. Photographer: G.P. Lewis.

A female worker trucking a load of boiled rags at a Scottish paper works, October 1918. Photographer: G.P. Lewis.

Woman worker preparing to feed a beating machine which prepares the pulp in the paper mill, Scotland, October 1918. Photographer: G.P. Lewis.

Paper mills being
fed pulp, Scotland,
October 1918.
Photographer:
G.P. Lewis.

Women operating a large industrial paper guillotine, Scotland, October 1918.
Photographer: G.P. Lewis.

Women checking the paper for quality before packing, Scotland, October 1918.
Photographer: G.P. Lewis.

The corrugating machine in a paper mill, Scotland, October 1918. Photographer:
G.P. Lewis.

Female yard workers unloading waste rolls of paper from a railway wagon.

Bailing area for paper.

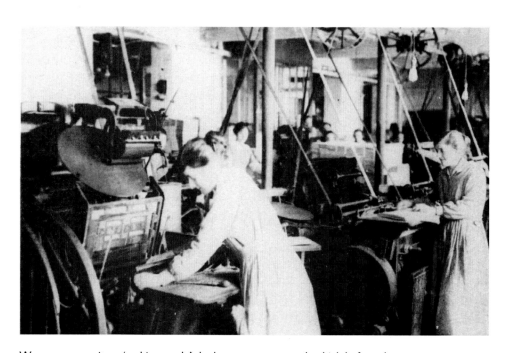

Women compositors 'making ready' the letter presses; work which before the war was exclusively a male occupation.

FOOD AND DRINK INDUSTRIES

Before 1914 women were confined to sack mending and light warehouse work in the grain-milling trade. In the larger bakeries, women were used to clean up and carry out light portering. In some biscuit factories they were employed on light manufacturing operations such as icing, decorating biscuits by hand, chocolate dipping, the lining of tins with paper and packing by hand. No women were employed in the brewing and malting industries' central operations before the war, although some women were employed in the bottling departments on bottle washing, stacking and packing.

In these trades, between 1914 and 1918, the percentage of women employed in the workforce rose from 35 per cent to 49 per cent, most of the increase due to women directly replacing men. The trades most affected were grain milling, bread and biscuit making and brewing. In the flour mills 7,800 women were introduced to men's work, being employed in such activities as sweeping, cleaning and packing, trucking and sack repair. There was vigorous opposition by the owners to the introduction of women and they only tolerated the use of women in the labour force due to the difficulties caused by the war. In brewing, women replaced 13,000 men filling casks (which was normally lads' work), weighing and breaking hops (men's work), cask and pulp washing, rinsing casks and testing. On light work it was reported by the brewers that a women in her 20s was regarded as being equal to a man; on heavy work three women were required to perform the work of two men. Often the companies introduced machinery to aid the heavy tasks, such as electric hoists to lift grain. In the bottling departments women were preferred to men and boys as they were considered to be more careful.

Before the war no women were employed in the brewing or maltings processes, or in the office at Samuel Allsopp and Sons, Burton. Girls had been employed in the bottling department, on bottle washing, stacking, examining and packing. During the war the position changed completely: women were employed in all areas. A similar story was reported by Ind Coope: before the war no women or girls were employed in the breweries; during the war women were employed in brewing, maltings, bottling, stores, cooperages and offices.

Vat-house workers cleaning the lager store casks, Cheshire, 1918.

Women brewery yard workers washing beer barrels for reuse, Cheshire, 1918.

Beer barrels being re-hooped by women, London, 1918.

Women coopers re-hooping and drilling the tap holes in beer barrels, London 1918.

Woman cooper re-hooping a barrel, London, 1918. During World War One there was considerable replacement of men by women in breweries in a wide range of unskilled processes such as cleaning, bottle washing and filling of bottles. Women also worked as cellar women and in the fermentation rooms. Coopering is a skilled trade, and before 1914 a woman cooper would have been unusual. Photographer Horace W. Nicholls titled the series of photographs he took 'Jolly Brewers'.

TEXTILE AND CLOTHING INDUSTRIES

The textile trades were largely a women's industry before World War One, employing two-fifths of all women who worked in industry, some four-fifths of the employees being female. In the cotton industries the work of cleaning and loosening the cotton fibres was done by men, while women were employed with men in the blowing and card room on machines laying the cotton fibres parallel. Spinning was done by men or women according to whether it was ring spinning or mule spinning. The majority of weavers were women working under the 'overlooking' of men. The weaver's work consisted almost entirely of keeping the shuttles furnished with cops of weft, placing the shuttles in the looms, replacing them by full ones as they became empty, repairing broken threads of the warp and stopping and starting the looms as the operators required. The number of looms worked by men was generally four, though in some districts they worked six with the assistance of a boy or girl known as a tenter. Women rarely worked more than four.

In the woollen and worsted trades the line of sex division was roughly the same as that of the cotton industry. As carried out in Yorkshire, men performed mule spinning and women were employed exclusively on yarn reeling and winding. In wool-combing, men on night shifts performed all the tasks normally carried out by women, who were not permitted to carry out night-shift work. During the day, men were restricted to card-grinding and bowl-minding, which were arduous, and wool drying, which was extremely hot work.

During the war the proportion of women in the textile industry rose from 58 per cent to 67 per cent. The actual numbers of women did not rise overall; the areas of dyeing, hosiery and bleaching expanded considerably during the war due to the requirements of the army and navy and absorbed large numbers of women; however, the period was also one which saw considerable shrinkage in the cotton industry. By 1918, there was substitution of men by women of around 60,000 within the industry. During the war, women replaced men by working on frame-machines and knitting-machines, and in pressing, boarding, stockroom and warehouse. Handknitting machines, which before the war were considered too heavy for women, were now operated by them. The work produced by the women was assessed as being equivalent to that of men's; despite this, the Employers' Federation were determined that pre-war division of labour would be revived and married women sent home.

Textile worker winding cotton from spools in a Nottingham lace factory, September 1918. Apart from domestic service, the largest pre-war employer of female labour was the textile industry. In 1914 some 836,000 women worked in the factories and mills centred on then traditional textile areas of Lancashire and Yorkshire. The lace industry saw a fall in demand during the war, in favour of more robust fabrics. In 1914, the industry employed 20,000 women; by 1918 the number employed had declined by a fifth. In contrast, the wider textile industry saw an increase in the numbers of women employed of 28,000, compared with a decline of 68,000 in the number of men. Photographer: G.P. Lewis.

Replacing empty spools, Nottingham, 1918.

Threading the bobbins, Nottingham, 1918.

Putting up a warp, Nottingham, 1918.

Putting up a thread on a lace-curtain machine, Nottingham, 1918.

Changing the jacquard cards on a Platferns
alcove lace machine, Nottingham, 1918.

Checking the threads on the lace-curtain
machine.

The mending room in a Nottingham lace factory. Natural light only was being used and so all the machines were arranged around the side of the room by the windows.

Lace workers with their teacher, Nottingham, 1918.

Finished lace articles.

Women loading the yarn on to a barrow.

Women workers attending the frames where the individual yarns form strands.

A stranding machine for producing house rope.

Women rope workers in a rope walk 170 fathoms in length.

Packing rope for the navy.

Baling the jute.

The warping
machines,
Weldon and
Wilkinson,
New Basford,
Nottingham.

Women trimming stockings.

Women trimming army socks, Weldon and Wilkinson.

Finishing area for trimming and inspecting army socks.

Warehouse workers in a wool sorting area.

Drying area for wool.

Carding machine in a wool factory.

SELECTED BIBLIOGRAPHY

Anderson, A., *Women in the Factory. 1893 to 1921* (London: John Murray, 1922).

Andrews, I.O., *The Economic Effects of the World War upon Women and Children in Great Britain.* Second edition (Oxford: Oxford University Press, 1921).

Bell, Lady F., *At the Works* (London, 1907).

Black, C. (ed.), *Married Women's Work* (London, 1915).

Booth, C., *Life and Labour of the People of London, 1892–1897* (London: Macmillan, 1902).

Braybon, G., *Women Workers in the First World War* (London: Routledge, 1989).

Burnett, J., *Useful Toil* (London: Allen Lane, 1974).

Drake, B., *Women in the Engineering Trades.* Fabian Research Paper (London, 1917).

Martindale, H., *Women Servants of the State, 1870–1938* (London: George Allen and Unwin, 1938).

Pankhurst, E.S., *The Home Front* (London: Hutchinson, 1932).

Pennington, S. and Westover, B. (eds), *A Hidden Workforce: Homeworkers in England, 1850–1985* (London: Macmillan, 1989).

Stone, G. (ed.), *Women War Workers* (London, 1917).

Government Papers

Health and Safety Inspectorate Annual Reports, 1913–1920.

War Cabinet Committee on Women in Industry, 1919. Cmd. 135 & 167.

Report of the Women's Advisory Committee on the Domestic Service Problem, 1919. Cmd. 67.

Web Resources

www.bbc.co.uk/history/0/ww1

www.bl.uk/world-war-one

www.nationalarchives.gov.uk/pathways/firstworldwar

www.1914.org

www.iwm.org.uk/history/first-world-war-home-front

www.english-heritage.org.uk/caring/first-world-war-home-front/remembrance

For additional information or to contact the author: womenfactoryworkww1@gmail.com

INDEX